Gaming the System

THE JOHN D. AND CATHERINE T. MACARTHUR FOUNDATION SERIES ON DIGITAL MEDIA AND LEARNING

Engineering Play: A Cultural History of Children's Software by Mizuko Ito

Hanging Out, Messing Around, and Geeking Out: Kids Living and Learning with New Media by Mizuko Ito, Sonja Baumer, Matteo Bittanti, danah boyd, Rachel Cody, Becky Herr-Stephenson, Heather A. Horst, Patricia G. Lange, Dilan Mahendran, Katynka Martínez, C. J. Pascoe, Dan Perkel, Laura Robinson, Christo Sims, Lisa Tripp, with contributions by Judd Antin, Megan Finn, Arthur Law, Annie Manion, Sarai Mitnick, David Schlossberg, and Sarita Yardi

The Civic Web: Young People, the Internet, and Civic Participation by Shakuntala Banaji and David Buckingham

Connected Play: Tweens in a Virtual World by Yasmin B. Kafai and Deborah A. Fields

The Digital Youth Network: Cultivating New Media Citizenship in Urban Communities edited by Brigid Barron, Kimberley Gomez, Nichole Pinkard, and Caitlin K. Martin

Connected Code: Children as the Programmers, Designers, and Makers for the 21st Century by Yasmin B. Kafai and Quinn Burke

The Interconnections Collection: Understanding Systems through Digital Design, developed by Kylie Peppler, Melissa Gresalfi, Katie Salen Tekinbaş, and Rafi Santo

> *Gaming the System: Designing with Gamestar Mechanic* by Katie Salen Tekinbaş, Melissa Gresalfi, Kylie Peppler, and Rafi Santo

> *Script Changers: Digital Storytelling with Scratch* by Kylie Peppler, Rafi Santo, Melissa Gresalfi, and Katie Salen Tekinbaş

> *Short Circuits: Crafting E-Puppets with DIY Electronics* by Kylie Peppler, Katie Salen Tekinbaş, Melissa Gresalfi, and Rafi Santo

> *Soft Circuits: Crafting E-Fashion with DIY Electronics* by Kylie Peppler, Melissa Gresalfi, Katie Salen Tekinbaş, and Rafi Santo

Inaugural Series Volumes

Six edited volumes were created through an interactive community review process and published online and in print in December 2007. They are the precursors to the peer-reviewed monographs in the series. For more information on these volumes, visit http://mitpress.mit.edu/books/series/john-d-and-catherine-t-macarthur-foundation-series-digital-media-and-learning.

Gaming the System
Designing with Gamestar Mechanic

Katie Salen Tekinbaş, Melissa Gresalfi,
Kylie Peppler, and Rafi Santo

The MIT Press
Cambridge, Massachusetts
London, England

MIT Press books may be purchased at special quantity discounts for business or sales promotional use. For information, please email special_sales@mitpress.mit.edu.

This book was set in Melior and Futura Std by the MIT Press. Printed and bound in the United States of America.

Library of Congress Cataloging-in-Publication Data
Tekinbaş, Katie Salen.
    Gaming the system : designing with Gamestar mechanic / Katie Salen Tekinbaş, Melissa Gresalfi, Kylie Peppler, and Rafi Santo.
        pages cm.—(The John D. and Catherine T. Macarthur Foundation series on digital media and learning)
    Includes bibliographical references and index.
    ISBN 978-0-262-02781-6 (hardcover : alk. paper) 1. Computer games—Design—Computer programs. 2. Computer games—Programming. 3. Gamestar mechanic. I. Gresalfi, Melissa, 1977–   II. Peppler, Kylie A.   III. Santo, Rafi, 1982–   IV. Title.
    QA76.76.C672T45 2014
    794.8'1536–dc23

                                        2014003647

10 9 8 7 6 5 4 3 2 1

CONTENTS

SERIES FOREWORD

In recent years, digital media and networks have become embedded in our everyday lives and are part of broad-based changes to how we engage in knowledge production, communication, and creative expression. Unlike the early years in the development of computers and computer-based media, digital media are now *commonplace* and *pervasive*, having been taken up by a wide range of individuals and institutions in all walks of life. Digital media have escaped the boundaries of professional and formal practice, and of the academic, governmental, and industry homes that initially fostered their development. Now they have been taken up by diverse populations and noninstitution-alized practices, including the peer activities of youth. Although specific forms of technology uptake are highly diverse, a generation is growing up in an era when digital media are part of the taken-for-granted social and cultural fabric of learning, play, and social communication.

This book series is founded upon the working hypothesis that those immersed in new digital tools and networks are engaged in an unprecedented exploration of language, games, social interaction, problem solving, and self-directed activity that leads to diverse forms of learning. These diverse forms of learning are reflected in expressions of identity, in how individuals express independence and creativity, and in their ability to learn, exercise judgment, and think systematically.

The defining frame for this series is not a particular theoretical or disciplinary approach, nor is it a fixed set of topics. Rather, the series revolves around a constellation of topics investigated from multiple disciplinary and practical frames. The series as a whole looks at the relation between youth, learning, and digital media, but each contribution to the series might deal with only a subset of this constellation. Erecting strict topical boundaries would exclude some of the most important work in the field. For example, restricting the content of the series only to people of a certain age would mean artificially reifying an age boundary when the phenomenon demands otherwise. This would become particularly problematic with new forms of online participation where one important outcome is the mixing of participants of different ages. The same goes for digital media, which are increasingly inseparable from analog and earlier media forms.

The series responds to certain changes in our media ecology that have important implications for learning. Specifically, these changes involve new forms of media *literacy* and developments in the modes of media *participation*. Digital media are part of a convergence between interactive media (most notably gaming), online networks, and existing media forms. Navigating this media ecology involves a palette of literacies that are being defined through practice but require more scholarly scrutiny before they can be fully incorporated pervasively into educational initiatives. Media literacy involves not only ways of understanding, interpreting, and critiquing media, but also the means for creative and social expression, online search and navigation, and a host of new technical skills. The potential gap in literacies and participation skills creates new challenges for educators who struggle to bridge media engagement inside and outside the classroom.

The John D. and Catherine T. MacArthur Foundation Series on Digital Media and Learning, published by the MIT Press, aims to close these gaps and provide innovative ways of thinking about and using new forms of knowledge production, communication, and creative expression.

FOREWORD

Today, we humans face massive problems because of complex systems. These are systems we have helped to create because of insufficient intelligence and care, systems like global warming, environmental degradation, broken governments, rapid technological change, national and global inequality, and global flows of immigrants fleeing war, poverty, and drought.

A *system* is any set of components or elements that are integrated, in the sense that to understand a system, we have to understand not just its elements (as a set), but also the ways in which they relate to each other to integrate into a whole that is more than the mere sum of its parts. A system can be simple, with only few elements and relations, or complex (complicated), with many elements and relationships. So, in one sense, a system can be said to be "complex" if it cannot be described easily because it has so many components and so many relationships and interactions among these components.

In mathematics and science, there is sometimes a more specific and technical meaning to the term *complex system*. In the technical sense, a system is complex if the inherent behavior of one or more components is nonlinear. Such systems are often said to be "sensitive to initial conditions" in the sense that very small changes in initial conditions will change the outcome of the system in such a way that we cannot predict the outcome of the system on any particular instance of it. Examples of such special complex systems include weather systems, global warming, the spread and evolution of viruses, markets, and the historical development of civilizations.

So what do video games have to do with complex systems? A *game* is a system of interacting rules that are normally invisible to the player. The player has to form hypotheses about these rules and how they interact in order to play the game strategically and well. This essentially means that strategic players form models of the rule system in their heads and test it in their play. This modeling can be tacit, or players can discuss it, debate it, and learn to articulate it in conversation with other players or on Internet game-based fan sites. This is model-based reasoning, the basis of science and the core way that we humans seek to understand and tame complexity.

Going further, players can "open the hood" of many games, looking at the program by which a game was designed. They are looking at the rules more directly now. If they want, they can "mod" them—that is, reprogram them and transform the game. When they do this, they are becoming designers, building and rebuilding systems as "tools for thought" and confronting the unintended consequences of their interventions. This is the basis of "design research" in terms of which scientists seek to design effective interventions into hard problems in the world.

Some systems in the world were not designed by humans (for example, weather). From time immemorial, storms were "acts of God," but now, thanks to human intervention, storms are increasingly the joint outcome of nature and humans. There are now fewer and fewer "natural systems" in which humans have not intervened. Other systems were designed explicitly by humans (for example, governments). More and more, it is important that we understand the interactions of humans as social beings with systems both designed and undesigned.

Games are important here, too, as they are inherently interactive systems between players and technology. Furthermore, the social aspect of games is taken further in modding and in interest-driven activities around games and gaming. Games as systems are more than software. They are linked software-social systems (what I have called "Big G Games").

Beyond the issue whether games—just as games—are good for developing systems thinking, games can have content that is about a system or systems thinking. This might be a game devoted to urban planning, complex machines, the spread of viruses, markets, the rise and fall of civilizations, or running an institution. Most games are not about systems; nonetheless, as systems that are "played," they invite systems thinking.

Gaming the System: Designing with Gamestar Mechanic is about a game that was explicitly designed to highlight the ability of games and game design to facilitate systems thinking. The game is a type of engaging Systems 101 course and is also meant to be good preparation for future learning in other areas of design and systems thinking. In that sense, it is a crucial intervention into our ongoing essential education for survival and human growth in the modern world.

James Paul Gee, Mary Lou Fulton Presidential Professor and Regents'
Professor of Literacy Studies, Arizona State University, james.gee@asu.edu

ACKNOWLEDGMENTS AND PROJECT HISTORY

ACKNOWLEDGMENTS

This book collection would not have been possible without the involvement of so many people, who were as inspired as we were by the idea of having youths develop powerful new ways for seeing and acting in the world. It's the result of years of collaboration with research and design partners across the United States, cycles of testing and feedback from teachers, and helpful insights from advisors and friends. In particular, we'd like to thank the following:

- Connie Yowell (Director of Education for U.S. Programs at the John D. and Catherine T. MacArthur Foundation), for the ongoing support provided to this project through the MacArthur Foundation's Digital Media and Learning (DML) initiative. The project would have been impossible without not only the funding provided, but also the incredible networks of colleagues within the DML field that she has done so much to foster.

- This material also is based in part upon work supported by the National Science Foundation under Grant No. 0855886, awarded to Kylie A. Peppler.

- Nichole Pinkard (Associate Professor of Interactive Media, Human Computer Interaction, and Education, DePaul University), for seeing the need for the project from the beginning and catalyzing this incredible group of partners to come together to work on it.

- The hard-working team of graduate research assistants at Indiana University who have contributed to this project over the years, including Sinem Siyyahan, Diane

Glosson, Charlene Volk, Mike Downton, Leon Gordon, Jackie Barnes, Sophia Bender, and Kate Shively, not to mention the broader Learning Sciences student body, who have all engaged in conversations with us around this work one way or another.

- Our colleagues and teacher leaders at the National Writing Project (NWP), who worked with us to pilot the activities in this book and helped us integrate their valuable insights into the final manuscript: Christina Cantrill, Paul Oh, Steve Moore, Lori Sue Garner, Janie Brown, Deidra Floyd, Laura Beth Fay, Carol Jehlen, Travis Powell, Laura Lee Stroud, Eric Tuck, Kevin Hodgson, Janelle Bence, Laura Fay Beth, Cliff Lee, Chad Sansing, and Trina Williams.

- The many institutions in Bloomington, Indiana, that have worked with us to pilot the activities in these books, including the Boys and Girls Club, under the leadership of Matthew Searle; and the Bloomington Project School, under the leadership of Daniel Baron.

- Our advisory board, which has provided valuable feedback both on the treatment of the ideas in these books and how they fit into the broader field: Linda Booth Sweeney, Natalie Rusk, Amon Millner, and Cindy Hmelo-Silver.

HISTORY OF THE GRINDING NEW LENSES PROJECT

One of the important lessons to be learned from working on systems thinking is that nothing is created in a vacuum; the same is true of all the work shared in this book. In this section, we briefly share the background on the Grinding New Lenses (GNL) project, which has led to this book collection and shaped its focus.

Taking a systems perspective, it's somewhat challenging to tell a linear story about what led to this work. But a good place to start might be a school called Quest to Learn (Q2L; q2l.org), which was opened by Katie Salen and Institute of Play in New York City in 2009 (www.instituteofplay.org) with support from the MacArthur Foundation's Digital Media and Learning initiative (Salen et al., 2010). The school was designed as a proof of concept to answer a unique question: How can school-based learning be designed based on powerful learning principles found in the best games—ones that inspire engagement, collaboration, critical thinking, and, of course, systems thinking?

In answering this question, Q2L did a number of things differently from traditional schools. To begin with, it reorganized the curriculum so that disciplines with natural intersections that were usually kept separate were joined together. Mathematics and English language arts became "Codeworlds," a class that focused on symbolic and representational systems. Another class called "The Way Things Work," taught science and math combined, and still another class called "Being, Space, and Place" was put together to teach history and English literature. Assessment and testing also was done differently—instead of finals at the end of each semester, each class broke up into teams that needed to work collaboratively on a week-long "boss level," which challenged the youths to integrate insights from the rest of the course. More broadly, the school made the idea of youths as designers and makers of systems central to the overall setup of Q2L's learning environment an idea that was reflected in the after-school activities, the course design, the boss levels, and the school's integration of design thinking throughout the curriculum. All the different parts of the school aimed to have kids use what they were learning to make or design something concrete.

While the Q2L school represented great innovations in learning and was lucky to have the freedom to do a lot of things differently, it was just one school. How could what was being learned there be shared, tested, and added to by the wealth of innovative educators and schools in the world already doing great work? In many ways, the GNL project, titled from the idea that systems thinking offers a powerful new "lens" to see the world, came from a desire to do just this. In the initiative, Kylie Peppler and Melissa Gresalfi, researchers and educational designers from Indiana University's Learning Sciences program (**education.indiana.edu/learnsci**), began to work with Katie Salen from Institute of Play (**instituteofplay.org**), Nichole Pinkard of DePaul University, and the Digital Youth Network (DYN; **digitalyouthnetwork.org**) to develop a series of modular toolkits that used the design of digital media as a means to develop systems thinking skills, all based on the existing approaches taken in the Q2L school. With the financial support of the MacArthur Foundation and the help of additional partners like the NWP (**nwp.org**), (a network of educators and local writing project sites that serve up to 100,000 teachers annually), the initiative worked for three years to make this idea a reality.

The main goal of the initiative was twofold: to create a series of scalable modular toolkits that used the power of designing with new media to promote engagement in design and systems thinking dispositions in young people; and to conduct research on what kind of curricular supports lead to the development of systems thinking dispositions through design activities.

Ultimately, four sets of modular curricula were developed in close coordination with teachers in the NWP network at every step of the process. Each of these uses a different technology and provides unique ways to engage in design with various approaches to understanding systems. The *Gaming the System* curricula involves game design with the Gamestar Mechanic (G*M) platform (Salen, 2007) and focuses on understanding games as systems and young people as designers of those systems. A second and third set of curricula, *Short Circuits* and *Soft Circuits,* use physical computing technology like light emitting diodes (LEDs), sensors, and the wearable technology controlled by the LilyPad Arduino (Buechley, 2006) to show how youths can create electronics embedded in paper, clothing, and other everyday objects and understand how these creations operate as systems. Finally, *Script Changers* focuses on the idea of using narrative and stories to understand systems, and uses the Scratch programming environment (Resnick et al., 2009) as a way to tell digital stories about systems by way of a computational system.

A key part of the process of developing these curricula was ensuring that the activities that we developed would be able to work in a variety of contexts and populations, and, in particular, be modifiable in ways that would let educators meet the distinct needs of their educational settings and populations. Whether they worked in after-school programs in places like Boys and Girls Clubs or science classrooms in rural public schools, with youths from marginalized backgrounds or privileged ones, we wanted to create something that was adaptable while remaining powerful. Therefore, a big part of the initiative involved testing and refining the modules in many different contexts over the course of two years.

Using an approach called Design-Based Research (DBR) (Brown, 1992), which employs approaches found in the world of engineering to engage in an iterative and cyclical design process around learning activities in which each implementation yields lessons that are incorporated into final designs, we piloted and tested the modules in many contexts. A particularly positive benefit of DBR is that it acknowledges that you're not necessarily going to get things right the first time (we certainly didn't!) but trusts a process of embracing failures and missteps as learning opportunities that are really gifts in disguise. For us, the process of being active learners about what worked and where was a central part of the work that we did in developing the activities being shared here.

Many of the activities were, as mentioned, initially developed and tested in New York City at Q2L; others were developed and piloted at local schools like the Bloomington Project School in Indiana, as well as at a local Boys and Girls Club that serves a wide range of youths from varied ethnic and socioeconomic backgrounds. A significant amount of testing was done in close coordination with our NWP partners in sites across the United States and through extended, project-specific summer workshops hosted at DePaul University in Chicago and elsewhere. Testing and refinement also was done in Chicago in schools affiliated with partners at the DYN. Additionally, DYN's parent institution, DePaul University, hosted a summer camp that served as a major testing ground for the curricula. Over the course of four weeks in the summer of 2011, expert teachers from across the United States affiliated with the NWP worked with researchers from Indiana University and designers from Institute of Play to refine the modules based on lessons born of implementing them with almost 100 youths native to Chicago, again with a mix of kids from different backgrounds. These educators are too numerous to list here, but their voices and contributions to this volume are recognized both in our list of contributors and in the "Voices from the Field" sections that you will see throughout all four of these volumes. The exercises, ideas, and guiding pedagogical ideas throughout these books are infused with their perspectives.

In developing the volumes, we wanted to ensure that the work was grounded both in insights from the academic literature on systems thinking and the learning sciences, and also in the lived experiences of educators. The research team contained a number of members who had worked as educators for many years in both formal learning contexts like public schools and informal ones like after-school programs, libraries, and museums. Most importantly, though, the initiative's partnership with the NWP meant that the kind of educators interested in the sort of innovative approaches that we were developing were kept at the center of our designs. They played important roles in testing and refining the modules as previously described, as well as serving on an editorial advisory board (including, most prominently, the assistance of Christina Cantrill, Paul Oh, and Steve Moore) that offered insights, made substantial edits, gave productive feedback, and helped to create many of the activities and materials found in these volumes. They were indispensable to the core design team throughout the project. Through this partnership, we hope that the current volumes are useful to educators in a wide variety of settings to engage youths in design activities that will help them to become systems thinkers, with the ultimate goal of transforming the world that we live in today.

As you might have already noticed, this project brought together many different participants with divergent backgrounds, including game designers from Institute of Play; researchers with backgrounds in the arts, mathematics, and civic education at Indiana University; out-of-school educators at DYN; and professional teachers from the NWP. So, what common threads brought all of these partners together? While there was certainly a common interest in systems thinking as a critical skill for an increasingly complex world, the group also shared a common belief that kids in the twenty-first century had new opportunities for learning as a result of the changing technological landscape. Like many forward-thinking educators, we all saw that the ways that we've been educating young people as a society, through focusing on skill and drill rather than innovation and exploration, and through teaching to the test rather than teaching to youths' interests, were doing a major disservice to young people.

Each of these partners was involved in a broader movement started by the MacArthur Foundation in 2006 to investigate the ways that digital media was changing how kids learned and how these technologies might be leveraged to create new opportunities for learning that might have been previously unimaginable. The Digital Media and Learning (DML) initiative has supported over $80 million in grants to research and develop innovations in digital learning at the time of this writing. It has focused on youth-interest-driven activity in digital spaces as a source of inspiration for creating new learning environments that incorporated the kinds of engagement and higher-order skill development found in places like massively multiplayer online games or do-it-yourself online creative communities like those centered around fan fiction, video blogging, and many other forms of making, tinkering, and designing. The Q2L school and the G*M platform used in the game design module were two examples of learning environments that came out of the DML initiative. Both aimed to build off of interests that youths already brought to school with them, as well as focus on the kinds of twenty-first-century skills they'll need to thrive in the world.

We share this background to enable the reader to think about the activities and resources in this collection not as an isolated approach to teaching, but rather as part of a larger movement to rethink learning in a digital age. There is an incredible amount of innovation happening at the edges of education, and in places that people tend not to think of as learning spaces. We see youths learning in new ways connected to pursuing their interests, engaging deeply, and solving problems through engagement with technology. We want to bring that kind of learning into more formal learning spaces, and we know that we're not alone in this desire. If you're reading this, it's probably because you agree with us that education can be done differently, that youths can engage in problems that are meaningful for them, are connected to their lives, and prepare them for lifelong learning in a changing and complex world.

A TEACHER'S REFLECTION

In concluding this section on the history of the project, we wanted to share the voice and experience of one of the many talented educators that worked on this project. Laura Lee Stroud—a secondary teacher and English language arts instructional coach in the Round Rock Independent School District, as well as a member of the Central Texas Writing Project—reflected on her experience as a maker and learner while engaging with the GNL curriculum during the GNL summer camp in 2011. As part of a playtesting moment, Stroud joined a number of other teachers to construct her own understanding of tools like G*M, Scratch, and e-textiles, as well as facilitate understanding for youths at the camp:

> The Grinding New Lenses camp experience was unlike any experience I'd ever had the opportunity to engage in. NWP teachers from all over the nation gathered for one month in Chicago, away from our homes and families, hoping to learn about systems thinking concepts and internalize them into our existing teaching repertoires. The only thing that we all knew about each

other and the work was that we believed in the lifelong learning process and that we had the NWP in common.

The group of educators, in partnership with researchers from Indiana University, Institute of Play, and the DYN, participated in conversations and activities that would evolve into the challenges described in these volumes. As the teachers explored platforms and tools in the service of systems thinking by doing what they soon would be asking youths to do, they also provided feedback, suggestions, and their own mods (modifications), contributing to the overall development of the modules as they exist today. As Stroud says, "As a professional, I was viewed as a professional and asked to help edit and revise the curriculum." This feedback and response process with the educators continued throughout the camp experience:

> After we were comfortable with the first layers of the curriculum we were to learn, we split into the modules we were to teach. We were partnered with another teacher and reviewed the materials, learned new vocabulary, and tried to familiarize ourselves with this newfound systems thinking perspective. Every day, in preparation for the summer camp youths, we processed the modules as learners and created the products—be it games, digital narratives with sprites as characters, or e-textile clothing and accessories.

Stroud was a facilitator of the *Soft Circuits* curriculum with youths, but also saw herself as a learner. By entering this brand new world of e-textiles (though it easily could have been a "brand new world of game development" or "brand new world of the programming of a digital story"), she discovered the gaps that existed in her own knowledge—about circuits and circuitry, for instance. This made her that much more sympathetic to the needs of her youths, which in turn allowed her to support them in relating the e-textiles work to their life experiences:

> As the youth entered the camps, for the most part not one teacher assumed the comfortable position of "expert" with our novice youths learning under us. Instead, we were positioned as learners alongside our campers. In some cases, our campers knew more about the content than did we the teachers. We had to remember our new value of supporter, encourager, observer, and researcher. We provided scaffolds for the new concepts, such as an immersion into the new vocabulary, and created a space in the modules for explicit vocabulary instruction. For example, the youths needed to know how to sew a "running stitch" before they could complete a circuit with conductive thread. In fact, in creating the e-cuff, we realized that many of the youths

had never made a hem, which is created with a running stitch. As we tried to explain to them how we teachers learned to sew a running stitch, a previously disinterested camper had a light bulb moment as she realized she in fact knew how to sew. She'd worked with her mother in a beauty shop in which they sewed in extra hair for clients. She not only knew how to create a running stitch, she was able to teach the other children how to do it, too! This experience reinforced for me the iterative process of discovering the strengths available within our classrooms that in turn make our instructional systems most productive.

Stroud concluded by saying:

When we teachers had group time to reflect on our experience, we found that we all struggled in one way or another and as a result we had a newfound level of respect for our youths' learning processes and struggles, as well as a wonderful glimpse into our own learning process.

LIST OF CONTRIBUTORS

Jackie Barnes, Indiana University
David Burton, Bloomington Project School
Christina Cantrill, National Writing Project
Avri Coleman, Digital Youth Network
Michael Downton, Indiana University
Deidra Floyd, Central Texas Writing Project
Leon Gordon, Indiana University
Katya Hott, E-Line Media
Steve Moore, Greater Kansas City Writing Project
Paul Oh, National Writing Project
Nichole Pinkard, DePaul University
Travis Powell, Oregon Writing Project
Scott Price, E-Line Media
Sinem Siyyahan, Arizona State University, Play2Connect Research Group
Charlene Volk, Indiana University
Scott Wallace, Bloomington Project School
Janis Watson, Indiana University
Malcolm Williams, Digital Youth Network

SYSTEMS THINKING CONCEPTS IN THIS BOOK COLLECTION

The goal of the *Interconnections: Understanding Systems through Digital Design* book collection is to make available an accessible set of activities that can help youths develop a "systems lens" for seeing the world—a lens they can use to make sense of problems around them. Our hope is that youths will be able to see, anticipate, and understand patterns in the systems that make up that world, and use those understandings to eventually design better systems.

In these modules, we share a range of practices and concepts related to systems thinking. These concepts by no means represent a comprehensive list of every major idea in systems thinking—instead, we have chosen to focus on a subset of key ideas that focus centrally on *understanding systems,* and, in some of the volumes, on more complex ideas related to *system dynamics.* Understanding systems involves recognizing the elements that structure a system, and, more important, the ways that those elements interconnect to impact each other and the overall function of a system. These understandings are mostly oriented toward analyzing a system at a particular point in time, which is a common focus in these modules. In contrast, the study of system dynamics is fundamentally concerned with understanding the behavior of systems *over time.* Examining how a system changes and the kinds of patterns that emerge over time is crucial to understanding how to intervene effectively in systems. As is detailed next, not all the modules deal with these ideas in the same way—the *Gaming the System* module focuses almost exclusively on supporting youths' understanding of systems, while the *Script Changers* module is more fundamentally concerned with understanding (and orchestrating) system changes over time.

The choices made about which concepts and practices to include were driven by the kinds of design activities that we envisioned for youths, and those ideas that are particularly easy to see via the tinkering and iteration processes associated with design. For example, all modules spend a significant amount of time helping youths to see the kinds of *interconnections* that take place among components of a system and the kinds of system dynamics that emerge through these interconnections. This focus is easily revealed through design work because youths can define interconnections, observe the functioning of the system, and then, through iterations on their designs, change the nature of these interconnections and immediately observe the resulting changes in system function. For example, when youths are designing a videogame (in *Gaming the System),* they can see immediately how changing the behavior of a single component (such as the health of an avatar, or the damage that an enemy can do) can immediately change how challenging the game is (the overall *function* of the game—the way it works). Likewise, in *Short Circuits* and *Soft Circuits,* youths can observe how changing the structure of light-emitting-diode (LED) connections (i.e., the ways that they're linked to each other) can immediately affect the number of LEDs that can light up.

Although there is a lot of overlap among the concepts covered in the four books, each one tackles these ideas uniquely, and there are some particular systems thinking concepts that are covered only in some modules. In the following sections, we describe and define the "big ideas" that are addressed in the modules. In the table that follows, the specifics of those big ideas and where they are addressed in each book and module are portrayed.

1. IDENTIFYING A SYSTEM.

Identifying a system and distinguishing it from other kinds of things that aren't systems. Specifically, a system is a collection of two or more components and processes that interconnect to function as a whole. Speed and comfort in a car for example are created by the interactions of the car's parts and thus are "greater than the sum" of all separate parts of the car. The way a system works is not the result of a single part but is produced by the *interaction* among the components and/or individual agents within it. A key way to differentiate things that are systems from things that aren't is to consider whether the overall way something works in the world will change if you remove one part of it.

2. USE LANGUAGE THAT REVEALS A SYSTEM'S CHARACTERISTICS AND FUNCTION.

A key indicator of youths' understanding of systems involves listening for the ways that they describe and make sense of a system. When using a systems thinking approach, youth will be able to identify a system's *components*, the *behaviors* of those components, how those behaviors are shaped by the *system's structure*, how these behaviors *interconnect* to form broader *system dynamics* which move the system towards a particular *function*. At times systems are designed to meet a particular *goal;* this goal can be (but is not always) aligned with the actual function of the system.

3. MAKE SYSTEMS VISIBLE.

When we learn to "make the system visible"—whether modeling a system on the back of a napkin, through a computer simulation, a game, a picture, a diagram, a set of mathematical computations, or a story—we can use these representations to communicate about how things work. At their best, good pictures of systems help both the creator and the "reader" or "audience" to understand not only the parts of the system (the components), but also, how those components work together to produce a whole.

4. SEEK OUT COMMON SYSTEM PATTERNS.

Beyond the core aspects of a system (i.e., components, behaviors, interconnections, dynamics, and functioning), there are a number of common patterns that are important for young people to look for when engaging with systems. Specifically, systems often have *reinforcing feedback loops* that cause growth or decline, as well as *balancing feedback loops* that create stability in a system. These loops are directly related to the *stocks and flows* of a system—what is coming into a system and what is going out. In particular, when more is flowing out of a system than is coming in, there begins to be a concern about *limited resources* within a system. Sometimes patterns in systems can be seen best by examining the ways that systems are *nested* within each other.

5. DESIGN AND INTERVENE IN SYSTEMS.

A key practice of a systems thinker involves both designing new systems and fixing systems that are out of balance. These interventions allow youths to go beyond simply interrogating existing systems in the world to use their understanding of how systems work to actually change the world around them, while doing so in a conscious way that respects the complexity of systems. The process of *designing* a system involves thinking deeply about the state of the system that you have envisioned, and how the particular components you have to work with might interconnect with other components for that state to be realized. This process of design involves more than understanding interconnections, however; it is also about considering what to do when things go wrong—the most productive *leverage point* to intervene or change a system, why a proposed solution might *fail*, and what *unintended consequences* might occur based on your design.

6. SHIFT PERSPECTIVES TO UNDERSTAND SYSTEMS.

Systems thinkers regularly shift perspectives as they look at systems to get the full picture of what's happening. They think about the actors in a system and what *mental models* they bring to the system that affect the way that they participate. They shift among different *levels of perspective*—from events, to patterns, to structures, and finally to the mental models that give rise to a system—to better understand that system. And finally, they change the *time horizon* associated with looking at a system in order to find *time delays* from prior actions in a system.

Legend for book columns:
- **G** = Gaming the System: Designing with Gamestar Mechanic (CH 1–6)
- **S** = Script Changers: Digital Storytelling with Scratch (CH 1–6)
- **Sh** = Short Circuits: Crafting e-Puppets with DIY Electronics (CH 1–4)
- **So** = Soft Circuits: Crafting e-Fashion with DIY Electronics (CH 1–4)

Category	Concept	G1	G2	G3	G4	G5	G6	S1	S2	S3	S4	S5	S6	Sh1	Sh2	Sh3	Sh4	So1	So2	So3	So4
1. Identify systems	Identifying the way that a system is functioning	x	x	x	x	x	x	x	x	x	x	x	x	x	x	x	x	x	x	x	x
	Distinguishing the goal of a system	x	x	x	x	x	x	x						x	x	x	x	x	x	x	x
2. Use language that reveals a system's characteristics and function	Identifying components	x	x	x	x	x	x	x	x	x	x	x	x	x	x	x	x	x	x	x	x
	Identifying behaviors	x	x	x	x	x	x	x	x	x	x	x	x	x	x	x	x	x	x	x	x
	Identifying interconnections	x	x	x	x	x	x	x	x	x	x	x	x	x	x	x	x	x	x	x	x
	Perceiving dynamics	x	x	x	x	x	x			x	x	x	x	x				x			
	Considering the role of system structure			x						x								x			x
3. Make systems visible	Reinforcing feedback loops										x										
	Vicious cycles										x										
	Virtuous cycles										x										
	Balancing feedback loops						x					x		x	x			x			
4. Seek out common system patterns	Stocks and flows																				x
	Limited resources in systems													x				x			
	Nested systems								x												
	Dynamic equilibrium																				x
5. Design and intervene in systems	Designing a system		x		x	x	x	x	x	x	x	x	x	x				x	x	x	x
	Fixes that fail											x									
	Leverage points																x		x		
	Unintended consequences												x								x
6. Shift perspectives to understand systems	Mental models								x	x										x	
	Levels of perspective									x											
	Time horizons and delays							x													

ALIGNMENT TO COMMON CORE STATE STANDARDS

The following tables represent an at-a-glance view of the alignment of Design Challenges from all four books in the *Interconnections: Understanding Systems through Digital Design* collection to relevant Common Core State Standards (CCSS) for English Language Arts and Literacy in History/Social Studies, Science and Technical Subjects. Only relevant standards are included in these tables. (For the complete list of standards, go to **www.corestandards.org/ELA-Literacy**.)

The Common Core State Standards for English Language Arts and Literacy in History/Social Studies, Science, and Technical Subjects are the result of an initiative to provide a shared national framework for literacy development to prepare youths for college and the workforce. The CCSS span kindergarten through twelfth grade, divided into three bands: K–5, 6–8, and 9–12. The CCSS may be thought of as a "staircase" of increasing complexity that details what youths should be expected to read and write, both in English and in targeted content areas. The CCSS are built upon a set of guiding "anchor standards" that evolve through grade-level progression and emphasize informational text and argumentative writing, particularly at the middle and high school levels. In addition, the CCSS include a strand that emphasizes literacy skills associated with production and distribution via technology.

For newcomers, a useful way to enter into the English Language Arts standards is to read the online About the Standards page at the CCSS website (**www.corestandards .org/about-the-standards**), and then read the anchor standards for each grade band, as well as for the content areas.

Through the Design Challenges, youths are introduced to a range of core skills and information that stretch their learning potential and build on prior knowledge. Expect them to encounter material described in the English Language Arts standards for reading informational text for key ideas and detail, as well as the integration of knowledge and ideas; for producing and distributing writing with technology; and for speaking and listening tasks that prepare youths for college and careers through comprehension and collaboration, as well as the presentation of knowledge and ideas.

Because the *Interconnections* collection presents curricula that engage youths in literacy practices that fall in the English Language Arts domain, as well as the domains of History/Social Studies and Science and Technical Subjects, the letter-number designation that accompanies each standard in the table aligns with the CCSS letter-number designation as follows:

- R—Reading Literature

- RI—Reading Informational Text

- W—Writing

- SL—Speaking & Listening

- RST—Reading in Science and Technical Subjects

- WHST—Writing in History/Social Studies, Science and Technical Subjects

The standards included in these tables serve as a guide through which the Design Challenges can be understood in conjunction with the CCSS. They do not represent an exhaustive list of all possible alignments, but rather those most prevalent and immediate to the central tasks.

Common Core English Language Arts Standards	Gaming the System: Designing with Gamestar Mechanic					
	CH 1	CH 2	CH 3	CH 4	CH 5	CH 6
R.6-12.7 (anchor standard) Integrate and evaluate content presented in diverse formats and media, including visually and quantitatively, as well as in words.	x					x
RI.7.3 Analyze the interactions between individuals, events, and ideas in a text (e.g., how ideas influence individuals or events, or how individuals influence ideas or events).						x
RI.7.7 Compare and contrast a text to an audio, video, or multimedia version of the text, analyzing each medium's portrayal of the subject (e.g. how the delivery of a speech affects the impact of the words).						x
RI.7.9 Analyze how two or more authors writing about the same topic shape their presentations of key information by emphasizing different evidence or advancing different interpretations of facts.	x			x	x	
W.6-8.3 Write narratives to develop real or imagined experiences or events using effective technique, relevant descriptive details, and well-structured event sequences.	x	x	x	x		
W.7.6 Use technology, including the Internet, to produce and publish writing and link to and cite sources as well as to interact and collaborate with others, including linking to and citing sources.						x
RST.6-8.3 Follow precisely a multistep procedure when carrying out experiments, taking measurements, or performing technical tasks.	x	x	x	x	x	
RST.6-8.4 Determine the meaning of symbols, key terms, and other domain-specific words and phrases as they are used in a specific scientific or technical context relevant to grades 6–8 texts and topics.						
RST.6-8.7 Integrate quantitative or technical information expressed in words in a text with a version of that information expressed visually (e.g., in a flowchart, diagram, model, graph or table).	x	x	x	x	x	x
RST.6-8.9 Compare and contrast the information gained from experiments, simulations, video, or multimedia sources with that gained from reading a text on the same topic.	x	x	x	x	x	x
RST.11-12.9 Synthesize information from a range of sources (e.g., texts, experiments, simulations) into a coherent understanding of a process, phenomenon, or concept, resolving conflicting information when possible.						x
SL.6-12.4 (anchor standard) Present information, findings, and supporting evidence such that listeners can follow the line of reasoning and the organization, development, and style are appropriate to task, purpose, and audience.	x	x	x	x	x	x
SL.7.5 Include multimedia components and visual displays in presentations to clarify claims and findings and emphasize salient points.	x	x	x	x	x	

Common Core English Language Arts Standards	Script Changers: Digital Storytelling with Scratch					
	CH 1	CH 2	CH 3	CH 4	CH 5	CH 6
R.6-12.3 (anchor standard) Analyze how and why individuals, events and ideas develop and interact over the course of a text.			x	x	x	x
R.6-12.7 (anchor standard) Integrate and evaluate content presented in diverse formats and media, including visually and quantitatively, as well as in words.	x	x	x	x	x	x
RI.7.3 Analyze the interactions between individuals, events, and ideas in a text (e.g., how ideas influence individuals or events, or how individuals influence ideas or events).		x	x	x	x	x
W.6-12.2 (anchor standard) Write informative/explanatory texts to examine and convey complex ideas and information clearly and accurately through the effective selection, organization, and analysis of content.		x	x	x	x	x
W.8.3 Write narratives to develop real or imagined experiences or events using effective technique, relevant descriptive details, and well-structured event sequences.	x					
W.8.6 Use technology, including the Internet, to produce and publish writing and present the relationships between information and ideas efficiently as well as to interact and collaborate with others.	x	x	x	x		x
W.8.7 Conduct short research projects to answer a question (including a self-generated question), drawing on several sources and generating additional related, focused questions that allow for multiple avenues of exploration.				x		x
W.6-12.7 (anchor standard) Conduct short as well as more sustained research projects based on focused questions, demonstrating understanding of the subject under investigation.		x	x	x	x	x
W.6-12.9 (anchor standard) Draw evidence from literary or informational texts to support analysis, reflection and research.			x	x	x	x
RST.6-8.3 Follow precisely a multistep procedure when carrying out experiments, taking measurements, or performing technical tasks.	x	x	x	x	x	x
RST.6-8.4 Determine the meaning of symbols, key terms, and other domain-specific words and phrases as they are used in a specific scientific or technical context relevant to grades 6–8 texts and topics.						
RST.6-8.7 Integrate quantitative or technical information expressed in words in a text with a version of that information expressed visually (e.g., in a flowchart, diagram, model, graph or table).		x	x	x		x

Common Core English Language Arts Standards	Script Changers: Digital Storytelling with Scratch					
	CH 1	CH 2	CH 3	CH 4	CH 5	CH 6
RST.11-12.9 Synthesize information from a range of sources (e.g., texts, experiments, simulations) into a coherent understanding of a process. phenomenon, or concept, resolving conflicting information when possible.						x
SL.7.2 Analyze the main ideas and supporting details presented in diverse media and formats (e.g., visually, quantitatively, orally) and explain how the ideas clarify a topic, text or issue under study.		x	x	x	x	x
SL.7.4 Present claims and findings, emphasizing salient points in a focused, coherent manner with pertinent descriptions, facts, details, and examples; use appropriate eye contact, adequate volume, and clear pronunciation.						
SL.6-12.4 (anchor standard) Present information, findings, and supporting evidence such that listeners can follow the line of reasoning and the organization, development, and style are appropriate to task, purpose, and audience.		x	x	x	x	x
SL.7.5 Include multimedia components and visual displays in presentations to clarify claims and findings and emphasize salient points.			x	x		x
WHST.6-8.4 Produce clear and coherent writing in which the development, organization, and style are appropriate to task, purpose, and audience.						x
WHST.6-8.5 With some guidance and support from peers and adults, develop and strengthen writing as needed by planning, revising, editing, rewriting, or trying a new approach, focusing on how well purpose and audience have been addressed.						x
WHST.6-8.6 Use technology, including the Internet, to produce and publish writing and present the relationships between information and ideas clearly and efficiently.						x
WHST.6-8.7 Conduct short research projects to answer a question (including a self-generated question), drawing on several sources and generating additional related, focused questions that allow for multiple avenues of exploration.			x			x

Common Core English Language Arts Standards	Short Circuits: Crafting e-Puppets with DIY Electronics				Soft Circuits: Crafting e-Fashion with DIY Electronics			
	CH 1	CH 2	CH 3	CH 4	CH 1	CH 2	CH 3	CH 4
R.6-12.7 (anchor standard) Integrate and evaluate content presented in diverse formats and media, including visually and quantitatively, as well as in words.				x				
RI.7.3 Analyze the interactions between individuals, events, and ideas in a text (e.g., how ideas influence individuals or events, or how individuals influence ideas or events).			x			x		
RI.7.4 Determine the meaning of words and phrases as they are used in a text, including figurative, connotative, and technical meanings; analyze the impact of a specific word choice on meaning and tone.						x		x
RI.7.5 Include multimedia components and visual displays in presentations to clarify claims and findings and emphasize salient points.			x				x	
RI.8.5 Analyze in detail the structure of a specific paragraph in a text, including the role of particular sentences in developing and refining a key concept							x	
RI.8.7 Evaluate the advantages and disadvantages of using different mediums (e.g., print or digital text, video, multimedia) to present a particular topic or idea							x	
W.6-12.2 (anchor standard) Write informative/explanatory texts to examine and convey complex ideas and information clearly and accurately through the effective selection, organization, and analysis of content.	x				x			
W.6-8.3 Write narratives to develop real or imagined experiences or events using effective technique, relevant descriptive details, and well-structured event sequences.		x			x			
W.7.6 Use technology, including the Internet, to produce and publish writing and link to and cite sources as well as to interact and collaborate with others, including linking to and citing sources.								x
W.8.6 Use technology, including the Internet, to produce and publish writing and present the relationships between information and ideas efficiently as well as to interact and collaborate with others.			x					
w.8.7 Conduct short research projects to answer a question (including a self-generated question), drawing on several sources and generating additional related, focused questions that allow for multiple avenues of exploration.							x	
rST.6-8.3 Follow precisely a multistep procedure when carrying out experiments, taking measurements, or performing technical tasks.		x			x			x
rST.6-8.4 Determine the meaning of symbols, key terms, and other domain-specific words and phrases as they are used in a specific scientific or technical context relevant to grades 6–8 texts and topics.		x				x		x
RST.6-8.7 Integrate quantitative or technical information expressed in words in a text with a version of that information expressed visually (e.g., in a flowchart, diagram, model, graph or table).	x				x			x

Common Core English Language Arts Standards	Short Circuits: Crafting e-Puppets with DIY Electronics				Soft Circuits: Crafting e-Fashion with DIY Electronics			
	CH 1	CH 2	CH 3	CH 4	CH 1	CH 2	CH 3	CH 4
RST.6-8.9 Compare and contrast the information gained from experiments, simulations, video, or multimedia sources with that gained from reading a text on the same topic.								x
RST.11-12.9 Synthesize information from a range of sources (e.g., texts, experiments, simulations) into a coherent understanding of a process, phenomenon, or concept, resolving conflicting information when possible.			x		x			
SL.6-12.4 (anchor standard) Present information, findings, and supporting evidence such that listeners can follow the line of reasoning and the organization, development, and style are appropriate to task, purpose, and audience.	x		x		x		x	
SL.7.2 Analyze the main ideas and supporting details presented in diverse media and formats (e.g., visually, quantitatively, orally) and explain how the ideas clarify a topic, text, or issue under study.						x		
SL.7.4 Present claims and findings, emphasizing salient points in a focused, coherent manner with pertinent descriptions, facts, details, and examples; use appropriate eye contact, adequate volume, and clear pronunciation.				x				
SL.7.5 Include multimedia components and visual displays in presentations to clarify claims and findings and emphasize salient points.			x			x		
WHST.6-8.4 Produce clear and coherent writing in which the development, organization, and style are appropriate to task, purpose, and audience.			x					x
WHST.6-8.6 Use technology, including the Internet, to produce and publish writing and present the relationships between information and ideas clearly and efficiently.							x	

NEXT GENERATION SCIENCE STANDARDS

Because the Interconnections book collection presents curricula that engage youths in design-oriented activities that embrace the sciences, the standards included in this table serve as a guide through which the challenges can be understood in conjunction with the Next Generation Science Standards (NGSS; found at **www.nextgenscience.org/ next-generation-science-standards**). They do not represent an exhaustive list of all possible alignments, but rather those most prevalent and immediate to the central tasks.

As the NGSS are explicit in assigning specific scientific topics and learning to specific grade levels, the correlations in these tables range from third grade to high school. The following tables were created to help identify which national science standards align to our Design Challenges, to what grade, and in which challenge each is addressed. Please note, however, that all the Design Challenges have been tested in a wide range of ability, grade, and age groups.

NGSS CODE DESIGNATIONS

- 3–5: Upper elementary grades
- MS: Middle school grades 6–8
- HS: High school grades 9–12
- ESS: Earth and Space Science
- ETS: Engineering, Technology, and Applications of Science
- PS: Physical Sciences

Next Generation Science Standards	Gaming the System: Designing with Gamestar Mechanic					
	CH 1	CH 2	CH 3	CH 4	CH 5	CH 6
ETS1 Engineering Design						
3-5-ETS1-1. Define a simple design problem reflecting a need or a want that includes specified criteria for success and constraints on materials, time, or cost.	x	x	x	x	x	x
3-5-ETS1-2. Generate and compare multiple possible solutions to a problem based on how well each is likely to meet the criteria and constraints of the problem.	x	x	x	x	x	x
3-5-ETS1-3. Plan and carry out fair tests in which variables are controlled and failure points are considered to identify aspects of a model or prototype that can be improved.	x	x	x	x	x	x
MS-ETS1-1. Define the criteria and constraints of a design problem with sufficient precision to ensure a successful solution, taking into account relevant scientific principles and potential impacts on people and the natural environment that may limit possible solutions.			x	x	x	x
MS-ETS1-2. Evaluate competing design solutions using a systematic process to determine how well they meet the criteria and constraints of the problem.	x	x	x	x	x	x
MS-ETS1-3. Analyze data from tests to determine similarities and differences among several design solutions to identify the best characteristics of each that can be combined into a new solution to better meet the criteria for success.				x	x	
MS-ETS1-4. Develop a model to generate data for iterative testing and modification of a proposed object, tool, or process such that an optimal design can be achieved.	x	x	x	x	x	x

Next Generation Science Standards

Script Changers: Digital Storytelling with Scratch						
	CH 1	CH 2	CH 3	CH 4	CH 5	CH 6
ETS1 Engineering Design						
3-5-ETS1-1. Define a simple design problem reflecting a need or a want that includes specified criteria for success and constraints on materials, time, or cost.	x	x		x	x	x
3-5-ETS1-2. Generate and compare multiple possible solutions to a problem based on how well each is likely to meet the criteria and constraints of the problem.			x	x	x	x
3-5-ETS1-3. Plan and carry out fair tests in which variables are controlled and failure points are considered to identify aspects of a model or prototype that can be improved.				x	x	x
MS-ETS1-1. Define the criteria and constraints of a design problem with sufficient precision to ensure a successful solution, taking into account relevant scientific principles and potential impacts on people and the natural environment that may limit possible solutions.	x	x	x	x	x	x
MS-ETS1-2. Evaluate competing design solutions using a systematic process to determine how well they meet the criteria and constraints of the problem.			x	x	x	x
MS-ETS1-3. Analyze data from tests to determine similarities and differences among several design solutions to identify the best characteristics of each that can be combined into a new solution to better meet the criteria for success.				x	x	x
MS-ETS1-4. Develop a model to generate data for iterative testing and modification of a proposed object, tool, or process such that an optimal design can be achieved.		x	x	x	x	x
ESS3 Human Impacts						
MS-ESS3-3. Apply scientific principles to design a method for monitoring and minimizing a human impact on the environment.			x	x	x	x

Next Generation Science Standards	Short Circuits: Crafting e-Puppets with DIY Electronics				Soft Circuits: Crafting e-Fashion with DIY Electronics			
	CH 1	CH 2	CH 3	CH 4	CH 1	CH 2	CH 3	CH 4
PS2 Motion and Stability: Forces and Interactions								
3-PS2-3. Ask questions to determine cause and effect relationships of electric or magnetic interactions between two objects not in contact with each other.	x	x	x	x	x	x	x	x
MS-PS2-3. Ask questions about data to determine the factors that affect the strength of electric and magnetic forces.	x	x	x	x	x	x	x	x
PS3 Energy								
4-PS3-2. Make observations to provide evidence that energy can be transferred from place to place by sound, light, heat, and electric currents.	x	x	x	x	x	x	x	x
4-PS3-4. Apply scientific ideas to design, test, and refine a device that converts energy from one form to another.	x	x	x	x	x	x		x
MS-PS3-2. Develop a model to describe that when the arrangement of objects interacting at a distance changes, different amounts of potential energy are stored in the system.		x				x		
HS-PS3-3. Design, build, and refine a device that works within given constraints to convert one form of energy into another form of energy.								x
ETS1 Engineering Design								
3-5-ETS1-1. Define a simple design problem reflecting a need or a want that includes specified criteria for success and constraints on materials, time, or cost.	x	x	x	x	x	x	x	x
3-5-ETS1-2. Generate and compare multiple possible solutions to a problem based on how well each is likely to meet the criteria and constraints of the problem.	x	x	x	x	x	x	x	x
3-5-ETS1-3. Plan and carry out fair tests in which variables are controlled and failure points are considered to identify aspects of a model or prototype that can be improved.	x	x	x	x	x	x	x	x
MS-ETS1-1. Define the criteria and constraints of a design problem with sufficient precision to ensure a successful solution, taking into account relevant scientific principles and potential impacts on people and the natural environment that may limit possible solutions.						x		
MS-ETS1-2. Evaluate competing design solutions using a systematic process to determine how well they meet the criteria and constraints of the problem.	x	x			x			
MS-ETS1-4. Develop a model to generate data for iterative testing and modification of a proposed object, tool, or process such that an optimal design can be achieved.		x		x		x	x	x

INTRODUCTION

You think that because you understand "one" that you must therefore understand "two" because one and one make two. But you forget that you must also understand "and."

—Sufi teaching

Few would argue with the idea that the world is growing more complex as the twenty-first century unfolds. We live in a time that not only requires us to work across disciplines to solve problems, but also one in which these problems are of unprecedented scale, coming from a world that is more interconnected than ever. In such a context, power rests in the hands of those who understand the nature of the interdependent systems that organize the world, and, more important, can identify where to act or how to intervene in order to change those systems. Effective intervention requires considering not just simple causal relations, but also the complex interconnections that work together in often-unexpected ways to produce an outcome. Taking action in our complex world requires a set of twenty-first century skills and competencies called "systems thinking."

Systems thinking is best characterized by the old dictum that the whole is always greater than the sum of its parts. It's an approach that involves considering not just the behavior of individual components of a system, but also the complex interconnections between multiple parts that work together to form a whole. Systems are ubiquitous in our world—which includes natural systems that deal with climate and biodiversity, economic systems that drive production and labor trends, and political systems that enact governance of communities and nations. And, of course, these systems are themselves connected to one another in important ways, so understanding the nature of these interconnections, not just within but also across systems, is becoming ever more vital. The promise of learning to reason about how systems work is that of creating a new and effective lens for seeing, engaging with, and changing the world.

Systems thinking allows one not just to understand better how systems function, but also to decide the best way to intervene to *change* systems. Systems thinkers have the potential to have a significant impact on the world around them—an impact that is often denied to those who think in simple cause-and-effect terms. As a consequence, we believe that to effectively and ethically educate children to thrive in the twenty-first century, we must create contexts in which young people are supported in learning to be creative and courageous about making changes to systems in the world and to understand that those changes will always have an impact on other parts of the system—everything is interconnected. It's not enough to instill this competency in current leaders—we must prepare the next generation to be effective and thoughtful stewards of the world that they will inherit soon. Helping young people to understand how systems work, how they are represented, and how they change—via direct or indirect means—is critically important to this larger project. Furthermore, it's important that young people learn about systems not in a distant and unfamiliar context, but in contexts that have meaning to today's youth— those rooted in popular culture, design, and new technologies. This approach is the basis of this collection.

Digital media are central in almost every aspect of daily life, most notably in how we communicate, understand political issues, reflect, (co-)produce, consume, and share knowledge. We are living in an era in which digital media is rapidly becoming a driving force in globalization, scientific advances, and the intersection of cultures. The growing accessibility of digital tools and networks, the prevalence of many-to-many distribution models, and the large-scale online aggregation of information and culture are leading to profound changes in how we create and access knowledge. Perhaps nowhere is this digital influence contested more than in education, where questions arise about the ability of traditional systems to prepare young people for the social, economic, and political demands of a complex and connected new century.

This collection, Interconnections: Understanding Systems through Digital Design, builds on the existing work of educators, management theorists, designers, and learning scientists who are aiming to promote systems thinking in young people. The project uses a design-based approach to learning and offers a toolkit for supporting systems thinking in ways that are aligned to current Common Core State Standards (CCSS) and relevant to youth interests in digital culture. Through a collaborative effort across a leading group of designers and educators from Institute of Play, Indiana University's Creativity Labs, the Digital Youth Network (DYN), and the National Writing Project (NWP), we've developed an innovative approach to supporting the development of systems thinking in young people; one that allows them to see how systems are at play in the digital contexts that they regularly engage with and one that puts them in the position of designers of those systems. Most prior work on teaching systems thinking has focused on the biological, physical, and social sciences. By contrast, this collection aligns itself with a growing body of work emerging from the fields of game design, digital storytelling, and do-it-yourself (DIY) electronics as contexts for engaging in systems thinking. Creating animated digital stories about aspects of their community they would like to see changed, for example, provides young people with rich opportunities for observation, analysis, and problem solving.

Each of the four books in the collection is rooted in *constructionist* learning theory, which positions young people as active creators of their own understanding by engaging in the design, iteration, and sharing of media artifacts within communities of interest (Papert, 1980; Kafai, 2006). Each book teaches systems thinking concepts and skills in the context of a specific digital media platform and includes an average of six design "challenges" totaling between 25 and 40+ hours of project time.

The first book in the collection, *Gaming the System: Designing with Gamestar Mechanic*, orients readers to the nature of games as systems, how game designers need to think in terms of complex interactions between game elements and rules, and how to involve systems concepts in the design process. The core curriculum uses Gamestar Mechanic (G*M), an online game design environment with a strong systems thinking focus. *Script Changers: Digital Storytelling with Scratch*, focuses on how stories offer an important lens for seeing the world as a series of systems and provides opportunities for young people to create interactive and animated stories about the systems around them. The projects in this book use the Scratch visual programming environment as a means to tell stories about how to affect change in youths' local communities. The two final books, *Short Circuits: Crafting e-Puppets with DIY Electronics* and *Soft Circuits: Crafting e-Fashion with DIY Electronics,* both explore the field of electronics and "e-textiles," which involves physical computing projects using fabrics and other everyday materials, including incorporating microprocessors into these materials and programming them with an accessible tool called Modkit.

WHAT IS SYSTEMS THINKING?

It has become increasingly clear that youths' experiences in school do not match the kinds of experiences that they are likely to have once they have completed school. The push to support "twenty-first-century" skills stems from this mismatch, and many have advocated for ensuring that young people learn to think about the world not as a simple set of cause-and-effect experiences, but rather as a set of complex systems. *Systems thinking* generally refers to a way of understanding the world as a set of systems that are made up of many components, each of which has distinct behaviors that change and interact, giving rise to emergent behavior. There are many advantages to understanding the world as a set of systems, but a chief one is that systems thinking allows youths to understand and interpret the world across content areas (Goldstone & Wilensky, 2008). Unfortunately, supporting youths to develop systems thinking has proven to be a significant challenge. First, systems thinking ideas are difficult (Hmelo-Silver & Pfeffer, 2004) and also can be counterintuitive (Wilensky & Resnick, 1999). Systems thinking requires youths to look for myriad contributions to system behaviors as opposed to simple cause-and-effect. Indeed, a key concept of systems thinking involves understanding that a small change can lead to a significant outcome—an idea that flies in the face of many core assumptions that we have about the world. Linda Booth Sweeney (2001) points out that most of our experiences in the world, particularly those we have as children, are explained in terms of linear causality. As a consequence, we have limited opportunities to practice talking about or interpreting our experience of the world as a set of systems.

Despite these challenges, the advantages to supporting youths to understand something about systems are clear. The open question is the best way to go about doing it. The *Gaming the System* module is designed based on findings that youths can learn about systems when they engage in tasks that require systems thinking to support their successful completion. Specifically, this module seeks to support development of youths' nascent understandings of systems thinking by building and experiencing systems for themselves. Our goal is to give youths opportunities to both create and be a part of systems through the design of computer games. We believe that this immersive involvement will help to ground their understanding of the world in experiences of complexity, rather than in the simple causal experiences that they generally have had.

While linking systems thinking to digital media and learning may seem novel, an integration of systems thinking in K–12 education began in the late 1980s and continues today through the efforts of many organizations and individuals, including the Waters Foundation, the Creative Learning Exchange, the Society for Organizational Learning Education Partnership, and various research groups at institutions like the Massachusetts Institute of Technology (MIT), Northwestern University, Rutgers, and Indiana University. There are also many passionate educators across the United States who have been informed by these initiatives, as well as by leaders in the field of systems dynamics, including Jay Forrester, Linda Booth Sweeney, Peter Senge, and George Richardson. According to Debra Lyneis of the Creative Learning Exchange, the field first began to take root in classrooms when Gordon Brown, a retired MIT dean of engineering, introduced a piece of modeling software called STELLA to a middle school teacher at Orange Grove Junior High School in Tucson, Arizona. That teacher, Frank Draper, and his principal, Mary Scheetz, worked for years to integrate systems thinking across grades in their school. The work was transformative, as Draper writes of his classroom experience:

Since October 1988 our classrooms have undergone an amazing transformation. Not only are we covering more material than just the required curriculum, but we are covering it faster (we will be through with the year's curriculum this week and will have to add more material to our curriculum for the remaining five weeks) and the students are learning more useful material than ever before. "Facts" are now anchored to meaning through the dynamic relationships they have with each other. In our classroom, students shift from being passive receptacles to active learners. They are not taught about science per se, but learn how to acquire and use knowledge (scientific and otherwise). Our jobs have shifted from dispensers of information to producers of environments that allow students to learn as much as possible.

We now see students come early to class (even early to school), stay after the bell rings, work through lunch, and work at home voluntarily (with no assignment given). When we work on a systems project—even when the students are working on the book research leading up to system work—there are essentially no motivation/discipline problems in our classrooms. (Draper, 1989)

At the same time, other initiatives rooted in digital media have used computer-based modeling and simulations as a powerful approach to teaching about systems. Leading designers have produced other kid-friendly modeling software packages such as StarLogo, NetLogo, and other tools to study the ways that these sorts of technologies can be used in the context of small and large groups in classrooms (Colella, Klopfer, & Resnick, 2001; Wilensky, 1999; Goldstone & Wilensky, 2008). The field also has extended its use of simulations to include participatory simulations (Colella, 2000) that use technology to allow youths to act as agents in simulations of complex systems. In addition, it has found ways to use simulation software to teach even children in early elementary classrooms the properties of complex systems (Danish et al., 2011).

Systems education now can be found in such diverse places as an elementary school in the Netherlands, public middle and high schools in New York City and Chicago, a private elementary day school in Toledo, a charter school in Chelmsford, Massachusetts, rural schools in northern Vermont and Georgia, suburban schools in Carlisle and Harvard, Massachusetts, and an entire school district in Tucson, Arizona. Some people believe that the middle school level is a good place to begin because of the developmental level of the youths and the flexibility of the middle school structure, but many (including Sweeney, 2001) advocate that both stories and simulations can be used to bring systems thinking to elementary schools, and others (including Lyneis, 2000) have developed robust systems thinking programs in high schools as well.

Throughout the process of coming to know something about their own capacity as systems thinkers, this book collection encourages educators and youths alike to manage and reflect on their evolving identities as learners, producers, peers, researchers, and citizens. The resulting focus is on learning how to *produce meaning*—both for themselves and for external audiences—within complex, multimodal, and systems-rich contexts. Creativity, expression, and innovation underlie this learning as learners practice and apply systems thinking concepts through the coding and decoding of linguistic, computational, social, and cultural systems. This approach challenges traditional barriers between consumer and producer/viewer and designer, allowing youths to gain the skills to act as full citizens within a connected, participatory landscape (Salen et al., 2010).

WHAT IDEAS ABOUT SYSTEMS WILL YOUTHS LEARN IN *GAMING THE SYSTEM*?

Although typically systems thinking curricula are concerned with encouraging youths to describe the behavior of systems, the goal of the *Gaming the System* module is for them to experience the internal structure and interconnections within systems. This is accomplished by creating design experiences that allow youths to tweak components of systems and examine the impact of those tweaks on other components of the system and on the overall function of the system as a whole. Specifically, our goal is that, by the end of the module, youths will have had opportunities to deeply engage with the following practices:

- **Identifying a system:** Understanding that a system is a collection of parts, or components, which interconnect to function as a whole.

- **Identifying how a system is functioning:** Understanding what a system is actually doing—the "state" that it is moving toward.

- **Distinguishing the goal of a system:** Identifying the ideal state or function of a system from the particular perspective of the designer.

- **Identifying components:** Considering what a system is composed of—what are the parts that work together to make a system function as it does?

- **Identifying behaviors:** Identifying the different ways that each component can act.

- **Identifying interconnections:** Identifying the different ways that a system's parts, or components, interact with each other through their behaviors and, through those interactions, change the behaviors of other elements.

- **Considering the role of system structure:** Understanding that the way the system works (i.e., what it actually does) is the product of a set of complex interconnections between components that cannot simply be reduced to an account of the components themselves—these sorts of system dynamics emerge from the way the components interconnect, and these interconnections largely are determined by the way that the system's structure sets them up in relation to one another.

- **Designing systems:** Students are participating in an iterative design process that involves designing systems, tweaking elements of those designs, creating new iterations, and then reflecting on how changes they made fundamentally shape the ways that those systems function and whether they satisfy their own goals for the system.

- **Modeling systems:** Students create versions of existing systems as designed games; that creation involves the act of translating what they understand about the target system to a new domain with new representations.

These are just a subset of the ideas relevant to systems thinking that are covered in the *Gaming the System* module. Each challenge details the ideas about systems thinking that are specifically covered. In addition, these ideas are explored in more depth in the "Delving Deeper into Systems Thinking" chapter that appears at the end of the Design Challenges.

WHAT IS DESIGN THINKING?

To know the world, one must construct it.
—Cesare Pavese

When a young person creates a video, a poster, an animation, a customized T-shirt, or a digital app, she is operating within the space of design. Design is a particularly important activity for learning because it positions the learner as an active agent in the creation process. As learners construct a public artifact, they externalize their mental models and iterate on them throughout the design process (Papert, 1980; Kafai, 2006). In contrast to prescriptive approaches to design, where youths all construct the same artifact in parallel or arrive at an idealized solution through design, the challenges in this book strike a balance between structure and free exploration (Colella, Klopfer, & Resnick, 2001). The activities presented here engage youths in design activities to encourage them to learn key systems thinking concepts. We also acknowledge that learning happens best when it's done in a collaborative setting and there are purposeful moments for reflection.

As such, the challenges in each volume share a common structure of activities, based on the creative design spiral proposed by Rusk, Resnick, and Cooke (2009).

Resnick describes the creative process of design as an idea that is realized by iteratively imagining, creating, playing, sharing, and reflecting on the work. *Imagining* begins with youths' open exploration of the materials to ignite their creativity and imagination to take the work in unexpected and personally meaningful directions. *Creating* places an emphasis on building, designing, and making artifacts that can be shared with a broader community. The act of construction not only provides opportunities to develop and enrich creative thinking, but also presents youths with the chance to experience disciplinary content through hands-on reconstruction of their prior knowledge. *Play*, the next step in the design cycle, is where playful experimentation with ideas is done in a low-risk environment to explore and test the boundaries of the materials. The public presentation or *sharing* of work in progress or completed work is also critical to the learning and motivation in the design process, where youths become more engaged and find new inspiration and an audience for their ideas. Resnick also argues for systematic *reflection* on both the design and learning process, where youths discuss and reflect on their thinking. Making

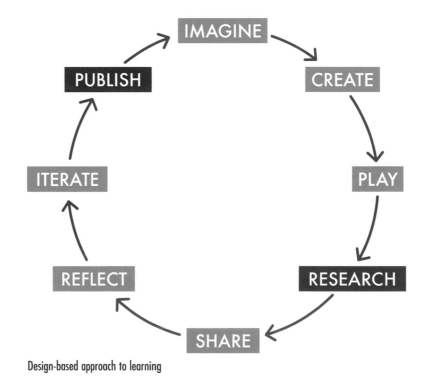

Design-based approach to learning

the thinking process visible through easy access to the design artifacts from various parts of the creative process is crucial to learning. Finally, Resnick describes this pathway through the design process as a spiral that is then iteratively repeated.

To this work, we add two more steps to the design cycle: Research and Publish. *Research* encapsulates the information gathering that is critical to high-quality teaching and learning. This includes the introduction and definition of key terms and vocabulary, the introduction of key concepts that are important to systems thinking and disciplinary content, and the activities used to gather this information (including the use of videos, diagrams, and other information sources). We also disentangle the sharing of the final product, which we call *Publish*, from more informal moments where sharing is done within the local community to assist in iteration. Current research has demonstrated that this is an important moment for learning and community building, and that there are some crucial differences in who is likely to post in the informal, interest-driven hours (Lenhart & Madden, 2007).

As a methodology for learning about systems, design is all about providing constructive contexts in which to explore ideas, interactions, and expressions. Linking design to digital media tools expands this context further: digital tools often make it easier, faster, and less risky to test ideas. There is no need to worry about wasting expensive materials, and erasing a mistake is as easy as clicking a mouse. The act of designing incorporates complex technical, linguistic, and symbolic elements from a variety of domains, at a variety of different levels, and for a variety of different purposes. Designers explicate and defend design ideas, describe design issues and user interactions at a meta-level, imagine new possibilities, create and test hypotheses, and reflect on the impact of each of their creations as a distinctive medium in relation to other media. And each of these involves a melding of technological, social, communicational, and artistic concerns in the framework of a form of scientific thinking in the broad sense of the term. Designers make and think about complex interactive systems, a characteristic activity today, both in the media and in science.

The challenges included within this book emphasize a process of prototyping and iteration based on a design methodology: youths envision new solutions to open-ended problems, work through multiple versions of any idea, integrate ongoing feedback into the learning process, and identify the strengths and weaknesses of both their processes and solutions. In some cases, youths may choose to build on previous solutions or approaches of their peers, seeing themselves as contributors to a larger body of collaboratively generated knowledge.

DESIGNING A SUPPORTIVE LEARNING ENVIRONMENT

Before sharing the Design Challenges that we've developed, it's important to provide a set of guiding design principles for creating a supportive learning environment that are never stated explicitly, but form the base assumptions about what kind of pedagogy they're aiming to promote. As you adapt (and appropriate, of course), the activities in this book, we hope that the principles here might help guide you.

A design-oriented experience, particularly one created to support systems understandings has to be … well, designed. The curriculum modules shared in this book focus on activity structures and learning outcomes—what learners might be doing, with what tools, and in what kinds of configurations. Young people must experience the activities robustly when they take into account a set of larger principles defining the qualities of the learning context itself. The principles outlined next help to structure a learning setting that is itself understood as a dynamic system—one where the interactions among learners and mentors, peers, resources, and social contexts has been considered and where specific attention has been paid to the ways in which these different relationships reinforce or amplify each other.

The principles are intended to offer suggestions for how the experience of learning might be designed to support the learning resources offered later in the book. Please note that the principles should be understood as working together within a system—that is, no single principle does much on its own. It is in the relationships between principles that the robustness of the system resides. For example, creating learning experiences where a challenge is ongoing likely will fail miserably if it doesn't also include feedback that is immediate and ongoing. Organizing a classroom environment where authority is shared, expertise is distributed, and a broad range of ways to participate is allowed matters only if there are also visible ways for learners to share and exchange expertise and discover resources. The whole is far greater than the sum of its parts. The fact that the principles are listed separately should be understood as a limitation of the page, not as a feature of the principles.

1. Everyone is a participant.

Create a shared culture and practice where everyone contributes. Design learning experiences that invite participation and provide many different ways for individuals and groups to contribute. Build in roles and supports for teachers, mentors, and instructors to act as translators and bridge-builders for learners across domains and contexts. Make sure that there are opportunities for participants (especially new participants) to lurk and leech (i.e., observe and borrow), and that peer-based exchange, like communication and sharing, is easy and reciprocal. Provide a diverse set of resources to support teaching and peer-to-peer mentorship activities, allowing youths with various forms of expertise to take on leadership roles.

2. Feedback is everywhere; iteration is assumed.

Encourage youths to assume that their first draft is never the final version—they should make something and then gather feedback, rather than waiting to share their creation until they "get it right." Feedback should include structures for guidance and mentorship, which may take place via the online communities associated with the modules, or in classroom, after-school, or home settings. Make sure that there are plenty of ways for participants to share their work in progress with their peers, solicit feedback, teach others how to do things, and reflect on their own learning. Provide opportunities for participants to incorporate feedback in iterative design cycles. One key aspect of this latter element is allowing every participant's contribution to be visible to everyone else in the group through frequent posting, sharing, group discussion, or a combination of the three. Utilize the tools associated with the module platform to enable communication and exchange between peers who may or may not be part of the same program or setting to broaden the kind of feedback that youths receive.

3. Create a need to know.

One of the more powerful features of challenge-based experiences is that they create a *need to know* by challenging youths to solve a problem whose resources are accessible but require work to find. They must develop expertise in order to access the resources, and they are motivated to do so either because they find the problem context itself engaging or because it connects to an existing interest or passion. Make sure that challenges are implemented within learning environments that support situated inquiry and discovery so that youths have rich contexts within which they can practice using concepts and content. As participants advance through a challenge, provide a diverse array of opportunities for them to build social and cultural capital around their progress. Allow youths to collaborate in many different ways as they explore different roles or identities related to the design project at hand.

4. Learning happens by doing.

Modules emphasize performance-based activities that give rise to authentic learning tasks. These experiences provide opportunities for participants to develop knowledge and understanding through direct discovery and engagement with a complex but well-ordered problem space. These spaces often require participants to figure out the nature of the problem space itself, rather than proposing a specific problem to be solved.

Make sure that learners have access to robust mechanisms for discoverability; a number of resources to support this type of inquiry are included in this volume (on Systems Thinking Concept cards and Gaming the System Challenge cards), while additional resources—peer-produced tutorials and other materials—should be easy to find, use, and share. Think of ways to situate challenges within a context that has meaning or relevance for participants, whether in peer, interest-driven, or academic contexts. Provide participants with multiple, overlapping opportunities to interact with experts and mentors who model expert identities associated with the problem space. Explore teaming and competing structures like competitions and collaborations that mix collaborative and competitive elements in the service of problem discovery and solving.

5. Create meaningful public contexts for sharing.

In addition to sharing and receiving feedback during the design and iteration cycles, encourage the sharing of final products and projects with both local and global audiences. Knowing that there will be an audience, especially one that youths care about, is motivating, but also promotes a sense of creating something with a particular audience in mind. This contrasts with creating things in a vacuum, which is too often the case in educational contexts.

Create infrastructures for youths to share their work, skills, and knowledge with others across networks. These channels might take the form of online public portfolios, streamed video or podcasts, student-led parent conferences, or public events where work is critiqued and displayed, to name only a few options. Allow participants to develop identities in contexts of their own choosing; create opportunities for the acquisition of status via achievements that are visible in a range of home, school, workplace, and peer group settings. Provide diverse forms of recognition and assessment, which might take varied forms, including prizes, badges, ranking, ratings, and reviews.

6. Encourage play and tinkering.

Youths often learn best by experimentation, tinkering, and doing things that might look like they're "wasting time." As much as possible, build in open-ended spaces for playing and tinkering with the tools, materials, and platforms in addition to more structured challenges. Invite interaction and inquiry into the limits and possibilities of the platform, media, or form in which youths are working. Support learners in defining goals that structure the nature of their interaction and inquiry from moment to moment, as well as over a longer term.

7. Position youths as change agents.

The whole process of design implies agency—that people are able to create innovative solutions in the face of problems, be they large or small. And a big idea behind a pedagogy of systems thinking is that young people who bring this lens to complex problems can envision better solutions than those who don't. Help youths reflect on the choices that they are making in the design or transformation of a system—empower them to see themselves as agents of change.

WHO IS THIS BOOK COLLECTION FOR?

These materials were designed for both in- and out-of-school spaces. Educators and mentors using the materials and tools in this book, such as G*M, do not need to be experts in game design. The activities in this book are designed to spur a range of interactions between young people and the digital platform or tool, as well as between peers. Educators should serve as facilitators for youth discussion, reflection, and ideation. The principles of systems thinking encourage young people to figure things out, put puzzle pieces together, look for similar patterns, and work together to ask questions and find answers across disciplines. The activities have been designed to invite young people to teach one another, because the act of playing and making products for each other (be they games, stories, or physical objects) places learning in a collaborative context. Youths can show others what they've discovered as they work on their projects, which provides an opportunity for them to act as experts. We recommend that educators try and support youths taking on these roles in the classroom, serving as teachers and mentors to their peers. (A handy summary sheet for site administrators can be found at the very end of the book.)

APPROACH TO CONVERSATION AND CRITIQUE IN THIS VOLUME

With the aim of creating a participatory environment where feedback is welcomed and iteration is assumed, several processes and protocols have been included that support productive conversation and critique within groups. For example, there are many points where youths share their work with each other, with the goal of getting feedback to refine and improve their designs. This can be a tricky endeavor, as they might be reluctant to let others see their work, and not all youths are practiced at offering feedback that goes beyond being simply laudatory or critical, to hit a point of being *constructively critical.* Although there are many ways to help them learn to find this "sweet spot" of feedback, in these Design Challenges, we encourage them to give a balance of "warm" and "cool" feedback to each other, taking turns as presenter and responder. In any community that does not have much experience providing constructive feedback and critique, the warm and cool feedback protocol can be a really effective tool. Next, we give details about this process, as well as a few related suggestions. All of these could be modeled and discussed beforehand with youths to support familiarity and ease of use.

Warm/cool feedback: This type of feedback begins with a few minutes of warm feedback from the responder, which should include comments about how the work presented seems to meet the desired goals. Next, the responder provides a few minutes of cool feedback, sometimes phrased in the form of reflective questions. Cool feedback may include perceived disconnects, gaps, or problems in attaining the goal. This is an opportunity to include suggestions for making changes as well. You might note that people feel encouraged to improve something that they have worked on when they feel *good* about it. A young designer, especially, can become discouraged without some positive feelings and compliments about the design.

Consider role-playing this, with you—the teacher or mentor—taking on the part of the partner receiving feedback. Ask for a volunteer to give you examples of feedback, starting with warm feedback and then moving to cool. When processing the results

WARM FEEDBACK

elements that work well
goals that were met
things to build on

COOL FEEDBACK

areas of wondering
gaps or disconnects
suggestions for improvement

afterward, focus first on what felt like helpful feedback. Then explore with the group what types of feedback seemed unhelpful. Provide examples of several feedback sentence starters that might lead to more constructive conversation. (e.g., "Have you thought about ...?" "What were you thinking when you ...?" "I was confused when ... Can you help me understand?")

"Yes, and ..." feedback: Another way to support youths in developing ideas together is to have them generate "Yes, and ..." feedback as opposed to "Yes, but ..." or negative feedback. This type of feedback reserves judgment, challenge, or dismissal, and instead focuses on refining the original idea that the youths generated. It is a technique often used in supporting iteration in a design process.

One way to demonstrate the difference between these two types of feedback is to create a silly or neutral situation in which one person presents an idea (such as "I think we should get rid of all money. We don't need it."), and then a larger group answers only with "Yes, but ..." feedback (e.g., "Yes, but how can we buy things online without money?"). Then ask the presenter to present the same idea again and have the larger group answer only with "Yes, and ..." feedback (e.g., "Yes, and then maybe we could then use [suggestion] when we want to buy something online."). Ask the presenter, and then the group, to describe the differences between the two experiences.

Response starters: At any given moment, not everyone in any community will agree completely about what's working or not working in a creative project. Sometimes this means that debate is necessary to clarify ideas, and healthy debate can support the development of critical thinking skills around systems at play in their communities. To help youths respond to each other civilly while still disagreeing—during both formal response times and informal collaborative work periods—you may want to post in the room a range of possible response starters that introduce disagreement respectfully, such as the following:

- "I see your point, and ..."

- "I am wondering about ..."

- "I understand that you see this as a way to ..., and from my perspective ..."

- "What if ...?"

- "Yes, and ..."

APPROACH TO ASSESSMENT IN THIS VOLUME

Assessment is designed to happen in three ways in these modules: informally, through *embedded discussions* within challenges; and formally, as *structured reflections* and design feedback in the challenges, and as *written assessments,* which can be administered as pre- and post-tests. Of course, all assessments can and should be used at the discretion of the educator. All of the assessment opportunities that we included here were designed to be formative, serving not just as an important opportunity for the educator to get information on how youths are learning, but for the youths themselves to gain insight into their own understanding of the key ideas being explored and the areas that they might want to work to improve.

With the goal of helping to prepare you to listen for and evaluate youths' understanding, we also include rubrics that offer an overview of what "novice" versus "expert" understanding of the concepts in each section would look like. These rubrics are intended to be used for instructional decision making, so that the educator can determine whether students are ready to move on, must talk more about a particular idea, or need more chances to show what they know.

Informal assessments are marked with this "Let's talk" icon. These assessments are designed to be formative and informal, in that they take place within the context of the Design Challenge as small-group or whole-group conversations. These conversations should serve both to help youths formalize some of the ideas that they've been working on and to create an opportunity for the educator to gauge what they understand about a particular idea.

Structured assessments, indicated by the "Hands on" icon, are times when youths write down and document what they understand about a particular idea. Structured assessments come in a variety of forms, such as a piece of peer feedback about another person's design, a sketch or diagram about a youth's own design, or perhaps a paragraph in which the youth reflects on a particular idea. These assessments are intended to help youths formalize their understanding of a particular idea and are designed to provide educators with a formal representation (i.e., a hard copy!) of what they understand about a particular idea at a particular time. If desired, these assessments can be graded and returned to youths as a means of tracking performance toward a grade in the context of classroom use.

Written assessments are given at the end of the module (and perhaps at the beginning, if the educator is interested in pre- and post-change information). The written assessment is designed to measure what youths have learned across the entire module, and it targets both youths' understanding of key systems thinking content and what they've learned about a particular technology platform.

Information about ways that students might reason about the content can be found in the *What to Expect* sections of each Design Challenge. We share the end points of student reasoning (novice and expert) but, of course, youths may be novices in one area while expert at others—or transitioning between. Thus, the goal of these rubrics is not to merely categorize youths' thinking, but rather to determine how they are thinking about the content to inform decisions about how to proceed, review, or intervene.

COMMON CORE STATE STANDARDS AND TIPS FOR INTEGRATION

You might be asking yourself: Why focus on the Common Core State Standards (CCSS) for English Language Arts in a book designed to support understanding of systems thinking concepts through the use of a computer program like G*M? What do computer programming and literacy have in common? You will find that the art of game design in these challenges involves a number of key literacy arenas.

The CCSS for English Language Arts and Literacy in History/Social Studies, Science, and Technical Subjects are the result of an initiative to provide a shared national framework for literacy development. The CCSS span kindergarten through twelfth grade and may be thought of as a "staircase" of increasing complexity for what youths should be expected to read and write, both in English and in targeted content areas. The CCSS are built upon a set of guiding "anchor standards" that evolve through grade-level progression and emphasize (particularly at the middle and high school levels) informational text and argumentative writing. The CCSS also include a strand that emphasizes literacy skills associated with production and distribution via technology.

The challenges in this book rely on youths' ability to *prototype*—that is, draft and revise in an iterative manner until they come up with a final product (a key skill in game design). During the prototyping process, youths chart ideas, devise plans, and then communicate those plans to their peers in small and large groups to receive and incorporate feedback. In addition, youths are asked to analyze "texts," such as explanatory videos, as they relate to particular systems thinking concepts that are manifested in real-world contexts, and then apply what they've understood to their own game design process. Youths are asked to write as part of the reflective process and as a way to demonstrate understanding. As mentioned previously, in these Design Challenges, youths will be involved in a number of key literacy arenas, such as speaking and listening, analyzing texts, and visual literacy, as outlined in the CCSS through anchor standards such as the following:

Speaking and Listening (Presentation of Knowledge and Ideas)

4. Present information, findings, and supporting evidence such that listeners can follow the line of reasoning and the organization, development, and style are appropriate to task, purpose, and audience.

5. Make strategic use of digital media and visual displays of data to express information and enhance understanding of presentations.

Reading (Integration of Knowledge and Ideas)

9. Analyze how two or more texts address similar themes or topics in order to build knowledge or to compare the approaches the authors take.

In addition, technology is woven throughout the standards as a way to gain knowledge, as something to be understood through critical media analysis, and as a means to produce and disseminate work. These standards are featured in a variety of ways within the challenges of the *Gaming the System* module. Youths employ technology tools to gain meaning—from online videos to the instructions needed to progress through G*M. But perhaps most important, youths use technology tools to *produce*, to create artifacts that demonstrate their knowledge. Knowledge of G*M coding practices—its own literacy, one might argue—as well as knowledge of a complex systems example like predator-prey relationships. As your youths engage in the task of understanding how to develop digital games that make manifest systems thinking concepts, they will be doing so via challenges in this book that offer a rich toolset of language arts literacy practices infused with digital media.

TOOLKIT

In this toolkit, we offer an explanation of why designing video games is a useful way to help youths learn about systems. We then present an introduction to the game and community platform Gamestar Mechanic (G*M), upon which the systems thinking and game Design Challenges in this curriculum are based.

Throughout, we encourage instructors to follow the spirit, rather than the letter, of what we include in these Design Challenges. Every learning environment is different—a classroom is dramatically different from a library space, which is also different from an after-school program. Every group of youths is different—tweens are not teens, kids who grew up in a city are different from kids that grew up in rural areas, immigrant youths are different from youths born in their country of residence. And every educator is different in terms of their style, history, and relationships to youths. So we don't assume that the activities that we share will ever (or should ever) be implemented in the exact same way in every context. We assume that these materials will be adapted, reinvented, and even improved in your own environments. This is part of why we spent a good deal of space talking about the "big ideas"—the concepts and principles that drove this work—in the introduction of this book. We didn't simply see this sort of background as something interesting and informative (though we hope it was); we offered it as tools that you could use to bring this work to life. We hope that when you inevitably adapt the activities that we share to fit your context and interests, you have a sense of what the spirit behind the activities is, and you have the opportunity to adapt the lessons (and even create new activities) with these key principles in mind. Thus, it is important to note that our suggestions about the timing of the activities, the assessment of youth thinking, and ideas for whole-class discussions can and should be modified to adapt to your unique context.

This book contains a sequence of six game design challenges that build upon core systems thinking concepts. All the Design Challenges can exist relatively independently, but they are written with the assumption that you have read or introduced prior Design Challenges into the sequence; therefore, some limited modifications must be made if the Design Challenges are done out of order or as stand-alone activities. The information in the table at the end of this chapter is intended to guide your decision-making process and inform the trajectory that you're planning.

WHAT IS GAMESTAR MECHANIC?

Gamestar Mechanic (G*M) is a project of Institute of Play, designed by Gamelab and published by E-Line Media with the goal of helping youths learn about the principles of game design through fixing, and then later designing, digital games. It was designed for upper elementary and middle school youths, but it is open (and accessible) to anyone. Using a set of digital objects that can be clicked and dragged onto a game space, the design tools of G*M are particularly accessible, as they require no programming skills whatsoever. As youths design different kinds of games, they use these tools to personalize and add complexity to their games. There is a tremendous number and diversity of elements that are available within the platform for youths to use in designing their games. These include a variety of backgrounds and parameters for modifying the game space, text input tools, choices around types of avatars and enemies, as well as tools to modify movement style and speed, health and strength, win conditions, and much more. This diversity means that an unlimited number of completely unique games can be created and shared.

G*M was created out of a unique collaboration that brought together a commercial game design company (Gamelab), a learning research group (the Games, Learning, and Society [GLS] group at the University of Wisconsin-Madison), teachers, and youths. The impetus for the collaboration was a recognition that while there was a growing interest on the part of youths to create games, few tools existed that enabled them to do this as easily as tools in other domains, like GarageBand or iMovie. Game-making tools at the time required participants to learn computer programming, which was proving too high a bar of entry for many. The project was originally funded by the MacArthur Foundation as part of their Digital Media and Learning initiative and was taken over from Gamelab by Institute of Play, who oversaw its charitable purposes mandate and developed the G*M Learning Guide. The Institute has partnered with E-Line Media to publish the game and provide additional development support. Institute of Play and E-Line Media are currently continuing to collaborate on developing new resources and features for the game.

Gaming the System Challenges at a Glance

	Targeted Systems Thinking Concepts	General Activities
Design Challenge 1: Introduction to Game Design (Time: 255 minutes)	• Identifying a system • Identify the way that a system is functioning • Distinguishing the goal of a system • Identifying components • Identifying behaviors • Identifying interconnections	• What is a game, and what makes a game good? • General introduction to game design • Collaborative board game design • Get started with G*M
Design Challenge 2: Designing Top-Down Games (Time: 125 minutes)	• Identifying a system • Identify the way that a system is functioning • Distinguishing the goal of a system • Identifying components • Identifying behaviors • Identifying interconnections • Make systems visible	• Play G*M • Learn about and design a top-down game • Playtest and refine games
Design Challenge 3: Designing Platform Games (Time: 185 minutes)	• Identifying a system • Identify the way that a system is functioning • Distinguishing the goal of a system • Identifying components • Identifying behaviors • Identifying interconnections • Considering the role of system structure • Make systems visible	• Learn about platform games and how they differ from top-down games • Design platform games • Playtest and refine games • Model a different system (and fix it) using the systems thinking ideas used in game design
Design Challenge 4: Balancing the Game (Time: 135 minutes)	• Identifying a system • Identify the way that a system is functioning • Distinguishing the goal of a system • Identifying components • Identifying behaviors • Identifying interconnections	• Create the easiest and the hardest game (and think about what makes the games easy and difficult) • Playtest and refine games
Design Challenge 5: Patterns and Movement (Time: 130 minutes)	• Identify the way that a system is functioning • Identifying components • Identifying behaviors • Identifying interconnections	• Learn about different enemy movements (and how they relate to spatial constraints) • Design games that take advantage of different enemy and space behaviors (and their interconnections) • Playtest and refine games
Design Challenge 6: Modeling a Predator-Prey System (Time: 125 minutes)	• Identifying a system • Identify the way that a system is functioning • Distinguishing the goal of a system • Identifying components • Identifying behaviors • Identifying interconnections • Make systems visible • Balancing feedback loops	• Learn about predator-prey relationships, and balancing feedback • Model a predator-prey relationship by designing a game • Playtest and refine games

G*M began with a belief that the practice and production of game design enables a type of reflection in action that supports good learning. This approach has been demonstrated over the years in the development of commercial products like Lego Mindstorms, as well as other open-source tools and programming languages like Logo, Squeak, Scratch, and Alice, which were designed to teach procedural thinking, problem solving, and logic by learning to program. Seymour Papert and Mitchel Resnick pioneered thinking about how learning a programming language can empower a person to model knowledge and to see the world as a system of interconnected parts. G*M builds on this approach not by teaching the language of *programming,* but the language of *game design.*

This distinction is quite important for several reasons. First, many excellent game-making software products exist already and have been used, in limited cases, by teachers in K–12 and university contexts. These tools have a proven track record of facilitating game production and have opened up the context of game making to those who are not professional game designers. Yet while each of these tools *enables* game design, none of them embed the practice of or thinking about game design explicitly within the experience. They often focus on game programming as the primary pedagogy. Within these tools, games emerge from a set of programming procedures: make the ball bounce against a wall—*Make a wall sprite and a ball sprite;* manipulate the ball—*Add Event > Event Selector > Mouse > Left button.*

G*M contrasts this approach by situating the making of games within a larger game world, where the making and modifying (termed *modding*) of games is not only the primary play mechanic or mode of interaction, but also the means by which game design thinking and practice are modeled and performed. Through a series of carefully scaffolded Design Challenges, players are introduced to the rules governing the behaviors and relationships between creatures and earn the ability to access the creature DNA to modify basic parameters like speed, movement pattern, intelligence, health, loops, and *conditionals* (if this, then that). Players enter and play the game from the point of view of design. For this reason, the language of game design opens the door to a broader range of learners and allows even the most novice users to begin designing immediately.

WHY USE GAMES IN A SYSTEMS THINKING CURRICULUM?

It is worth noting why we have chosen to focus on game design in the *Gaming the System* module. First and foremost, games themselves are systems. The goal of the game is driven fundamentally by interconnections among components of the game. This is not only true for computer games like G*M, but for any kind of game that you can imagine. Central to making all games function is a set of interconnections among components—the components can be simple, such as in the game of solitaire, which includes cards, rules, and an individual player; or much more complex, such as in the game of Monopoly, which features a board; several players; several different board components, including dice, figures, cards, houses, and funds; and even rules that change over time.

Second, we chose games because we wanted youths to have opportunities to focus on the complexity of the way systems work without getting lost in the specifics of systems that could be foreign to them. There are many complex systems in the world—global climate, microchemical reactions, weather patterns, the human body ... the list goes on and on. Understanding how those systems work requires learning about the specific mechanisms that are in play in the system—that is, not only looking for characteristics of systems (e.g., identifying components, their behaviors, and their interconnections), but also learning disciplinary content that would allow one to actually understand and explain how components in these systems interconnect. By choosing to work with games, we have chosen a content area that youths are already very familiar with—indeed, often experts at—which allows them to focus on interconnections and system functioning, rather than needing to become immersed in particular disciplinary content that would be required to explain those same kinds of interconnections.

Finally, we chose games—specifically *designing* games—because we wanted youths to have a chance to build systems and then experience changing a component of that system and observing the consequences of that decision in real time. The best way to understand how behaviors of components affect the behaviors of other components is to see for yourself. In the *Gaming the System* module, youths have many opportunities to design, change, reflect, redesign, and play. In this context, making changes is as easy as clicking a button, and observing the consequences of those changes is merely a matter of playing the game again. This allows iterations to happen quickly and, more important, multiple times, allowing youths to begin to develop more robust understandings of the ways that interconnections affect the ultimate function of their game. One of the general challenges of learning about complex systems is that the results of actions are not so easy to see over time—the causes can be hidden. By putting youths into a situation where they're designing systems and are able to isolate how certain design decisions affect overall system behavior, we're preparing them to think better about how to intervene in systems in a more general sense.

TECHNICAL INFORMATION

WHERE DO YOU ACCESS THE G*M PROGRAM?

gamestarmechanic.com

WHAT ARE THE TECHNICAL REQUIREMENTS?

To use the G*M program, there are certain technical prerequisites. Because the software is web-based, youths must have access to at least one computer with Internet access and permission to contact the gamestarmechanic.com site. The computer also must have the Flash 10 player installed, which can be downloaded for free from adobe.com. If the Flash 10 player is not installed, you will get a prompt to install it automatically upon visiting the front page of the program. No additional purchases or downloads are required.

All modules in this book were created using the free version of the game, which includes specific "challenges" that you can access with through the following URL: gamestarmechanic.com/?activation=GAMINGTHESYSTEM. You also have the option of purchasing the Premium Educational package version of the game, which includes more features to help you manage your group, plus more content for you and the youths. Some of the features are as follows:

- Youths can customize their games with their own art

- Professional training (via a live webinar)

- Tools for managing youths' accounts

- Tools for tracking youths' activities and assessing their progress

- Higher levels of customer and technical support

- The option of having a private "walled" online community for your organization

Register New Account

Username
_____
(letters and numbers)
Other mechanics will see your username all around Gamestar Mechanic

Password
_____

Confirm Password
_____

Your Birthday
Month ⬍ | Day ⬍ | Year ⬍
Why do we ask for this?

NEXT

Register New Account - Step 2

Please enter your email address. We'll send a message to this address with instructions on how to activate your account, and we'll only use your email address to send you information about Gamestar Mechanic and for customer support. Privacy Policy

Email Address
_____

Confirm Email
_____

☐ I have read and accept the Terms of Service

☑ Please send me email about new Gamestar Mechanic features, contests and promotions

Type the letters and numbers into the box below

NEXT

Find out more about the premium version here: **gamestarmechanic.com/ teachers/faq**. Next, we include information about gaining access to the game and getting youths set up.

CREATING ACCOUNTS

Before using G*M, you and the youths will need to go through the registration process for new users. There are four steps, the third of which involves the receipt of an e-mail with an activation link to complete the process.

To register a large number of youths:

1. Create an account for yourself at **gamestarmechanic.com**.

2. Create an institution at **gamestarmechanic.com/teachers/setup**. This will create a "realm" within the game populated by only the youths you are working with.

3. Have the youths create their own accounts using the link provided to you during the institution setup.

4. Gain special access to two G*M experiences that were designed especially for *Gaming the System* by redeeming through a special URL within G*M. Once youths have created their account and logged in, direct them to follow this link: **gamestarmechanic.com/?activation=GAMINGTHESYSTEM**. If they are still logged in, they will simply need to click on the "redeem" button. If they have logged out, they will be prompted to log back in, and then asked to click on the "redeem" button. They will need this access in several of the Design Challenges of this book.

If you run into problems, e-mail **educators@gamestarmechanic.com**. Someone will follow up with you and help you with your problem.

AGE RANGE

The target audience for G*M is youths in the fourth to ninth grades, but that segment is by no means restrictive. It is designed to appeal to both boys and girls and does not assume any prior game design or programming experience for the youths. It is not particularly reading-heavy, and, due in part to heavy graphical support, it can be engaged in by youth at a broad range of reading levels.

WHAT DO YOUTHS DO IN G*M?

G*M affords youths opportunities to play, design, and share video games. Youths *play* through the "Quest," a narrative adventure shown in motion-comics and mini-games. Players complete quests with the goal of helping to save the world from a rogue game designer. As they move through the story, they encounter "broken" games that they must edit and fix. By playing and fixing games they earn sprites that they can use to *design* games in their workshop. They make their own games using drag-and-drop tools without having to learn complex computer programming language, reducing barriers to the game design process. They then can *share* their games in Game Alley, a community where youths review and comment on each other's games. In Game Alley, youths can see how others are playing their games with both qualitative (peer feedback) and quantitative (statistics) reactions. (**gamestarmechanic.com/game/alley**)

HOW DO TEACHERS USE G*M?

Teachers use G*M in many ways, including but not limited to the following:

- **Model systems:** A science teacher may have youths design games that model natural systems, like the water cycle or a specific ecosystem.
- **Tell stories:** An art teacher may have youths design games with specific visual or narrative qualities.
- **Teach game design:** A technology teacher may have youths design games that focus on games as systems, solving problems in games, or both.

BEYOND THE CHALLENGES: STRUCTURE OF G*M

As noted above, the specific Design Challenges that youths need to complete as part of this module can be found by accessing the link **gamestarmechanic.com/?activation=GAMINGTHESYSTEM**, and then by selecting specific challenges in the Workshop (as detailed in each Design Challenge in this book). Next, we describe the elements of G*M that are relevant to these Design Challenges.

G*M has three parts: Quest, Workshop, and Game Alley.

- *Quest* is a single-player storyline where youths earn *sprites*, the components that they can use to make their games. (**gamestarmechanic.com/quest**)

- The *Workshop* is where youths make their own games. (**gamestarmechanic .com/workshop**)

- *Game Alley* is where youths share their games in an online community. (**gamestar mechanic.com/game/alley**)

Youths will not need to complete quests if they are accessing G*M through the provided link. Quests are available to them, however, and they are an enjoyable way to help youths engage with key ideas of game design.

WORKSHOP

The *Workshop* is where players design games with their Toolbox and sprites. Each player starts with a default set of sprites to design with and earns more as he or she advances through the Quest. Players also have access to Template Games, which include sets of sprites; these templates provide nicely constrained design spaces that help youths focus on key ideas without getting lost in a plethora of sprite choices.

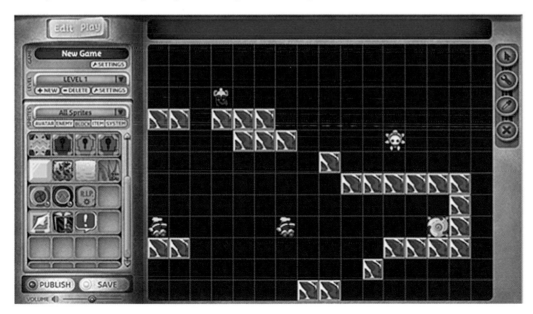

Toolbox   The *Toolbox* is the free-form game creation area of G*M accessed from within the Workshop, where users can build new games from scratch. The Toolbox has six components: *Game Grid, Sprite Tray, Tools, Edit/Play* toggle switch, *Level Settings,* and *Game Settings.*

Game Grid   The *Game Grid* is the work area where players can create their own games.

Sprite Tray Menus   There are two main sections in the *Sprite Tray.* At the top are levels and sprites. *Levels* in the current game are displayed, and the player can move freely between them to edit them. Clicking and dragging the level name to a new position within the window allows players to reorder the levels in their game. The Sprite Tray also contains all of the player's *sprites.*

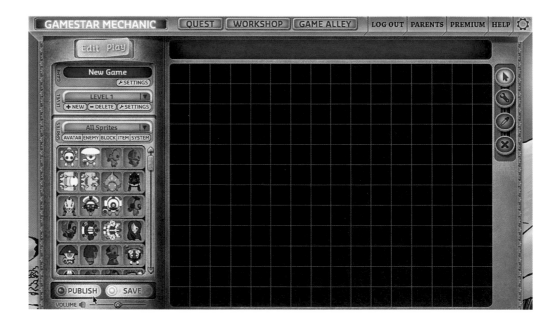

Sprites are the essential building blocks of G*M games. As players proceed through the Quests (in-game curricula), they are awarded new sprites to use in their games. Once a player has earned a sprite, it can be used an unlimited number of times. Earned sprites appear in the player's Work Area inventory. The more advanced a player is, the more sprites that he or she will have to choose among when building games. There are five kinds of sprites: *avatars* (the representation of the player), *enemies* (bad guys who can damage you), *blocks* (cubes that divide up the game space), *items* (functional and non-functional components that can be added to the game), and *system sprites* (which define certain goal conditions for the game, like timers, point counters, or frag counters).

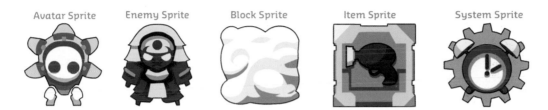

Avatar Sprite   Enemy Sprite   Block Sprite   Item Sprite   System Sprite

Tools Tools allow youths to manipulate the sprites they have selected. The available tools are as follows:

- When the *Arrow* tool is selected, designers can drag sprites out of their inventory to the grid, as well as picking up and dropping sprites that have been placed.

- The *Wrench* tool allows designers to change the parameters of the sprites that they have placed. Each sprite has an individual set of parameters that govern its behavior. These parameters include things like movement speed, damage, point value, etc.

- The *Eyedropper* tool allows designers to copy sprites that are placed on the grid. This is especially useful when the designer has changed the parameters of the sprite with the Wrench tool, because using the Eyedropper will create a clone of the sprite with the changed parameters, which makes it easy to duplicate customized sprites.

- The *X* tool allows designers to delete sprites placed on the playfield. This action is permanent.

Edit/Play Toggle   The *Edit/Play* toggle switch at the top of the Sprite Tray controls the behavior of the console. In *Edit* mode, the game is not "playing"—everything stands still. In *Play* mode, the mechanic can test that his or her game is working as intended. We recommend encouraging designers to test their games frequently.

Level Settings   Every game is composed of one or more levels. A *level* is a self-contained unit of game play with a defined goal. Think of this window as defining the "world" that the game takes place in. The Level Settings are used to control the overall qualities of the game space, including the perspective of the camera and the size of the level. Users can choose and adjust a variety of parameters that define this space. The first three fields in the Level Settings window allow the user to create a name for the level, write text that is displayed when a player begins playing the level, and write text that is displayed when players complete it.

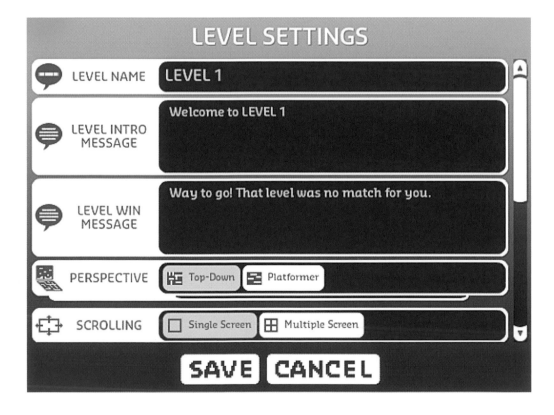

The *Perspective* of a level indicates whether the player is viewing the play field from either a *top-down* or *platform* (also called *side-scroller*) perspective. In the platform perspective, the player controls an avatar that jumps from platform to platform. In top-down perspective, the player controls an avatar seen from above that can move in all four directions.

Choosing the platform perspective opens up a *Gravity* submenu which is available only in this perspective, not in top-down games. Gravity determines the amount of downward force placed on moving sprites in the game. Increasing the gravity increases the speed at which objects fall; decreasing it allows avatar sprites to jump higher and fly.

Single Screen means that the game is restricted to the size of one visible game screen—a 16 x 12 grid of sprites. We recommend starting with this setting, as it can help new game designers to stay focused. This setting is available in both the platform and top-down perspectives. Choosing Single Screen opens a *Wraparound* submenu, which means that when the player moves past an edge of the playfield, his or her avatar will reappear at the opposite edge.

Multiple Screen means that the game screen (or the "camera") will move as the players move, revealing previously unseen areas as they move toward the edges. Choosing this option opens a submenu that lets users determine the total size of the playing field, up to a grid of 10 screens wide by 10 screens tall. This setting is available for both platform and top-down perspectives, but it leads to more complex design decisions, so we recommend it for advanced game mechanics.

Edge Bounding determines how the edges of the playfield behave. Some edges can stop forward motion or allow players to pass freely. In platform perspective, if players fall off the edge of the screen, they automatically lose the game.

Background and Music mode lets the user choose from background art and musical themes (or silence) that will play during the level. Mechanics start with a few of these and earn more throughout the various Quests. To see where in the Quests specific backgrounds and music are earned, go to the Quest Guide: **tinyurl.com/gsmlg-intro-questguide**.

Game Settings   Designers use *Game Settings* to write the text that players will see. This includes the *Game Name;* the *Game Intro Text,* which appears when the game is first opened; and the *Game Win Message,* which appears at the end of a game.

There are two other settings here that afford opportunities for teaching writing skills. *Goals and Rules* is a text area where designers can write what their game is about, and it is a good place to communicate the metaphor of a creative game. *Tips and Tricks* is a section where hints and other strategies for play can be shared. It is a good place for designers to think about what their players need to know and to practice didactic writing skills.

GAME ALLEY

Once games are published, they appear in Game Alley for other mechanics and visitors to the site to play. At the top of the Game Alley screen is the "Featured Challenge," which spotlights a Design Challenge that designers can take to demonstrate their design skills within a carefully chosen set of design goals. Games that result from a Design Challenge have the opportunity to be featured specially within the site.

Sharing, Feedback, and Embedding Games in Other Websites   Game Alley is also where players can review or comment on each other's games and provide helpful critical feedback as part of the iterative design process. These reviews have both *Ratings* and simple *Review Headings* to guide feedback.

Players can *share* a game by linking it, emailing it, embedding it into another website, or marking it as a favorite. Sharing a game will make it available even to people who are not logged in to G*M, so that players can show their games to their parents and friends, even if they don't have G*M accounts.

Reviews and comments are moderated. The Flag button will allow you to report unacceptable or inappropriate comments to the moderators.

DESIGN CHALLENGES OVERVIEW

CONTENTS

DESIGN CHALLENGE 1: INTRODUCTION TO GAMES AND GAME DESIGN

Total time: 280 minutes

The goal of the first challenge is to introduce youths to key concepts and vocabulary related to games and game design through playing and analyzing digital and non-digital games, as well as through classroom discussions. Specifically, youths will start to think about games as systems that are made up of components, each with its own behavior, which interconnect in order to form the overall way that the system functions. Youths will start by playing a non-digital game and analyzing the game as a system. Then they will have the opportunity to participate in collaborative game design. Working in groups, youth will design, play, and revise a board game using the U-Build Sorry! kit or by an alternative found-object game design activity. The challenge ends with youths playing Gamestar Mechanic (G*M), coming up with their own game ideas and sharing them with the whole group.

DESIGN CHALLENGE 2: DESIGNING TOP-DOWN GAMES

Total time: 125 minutes

The goal of this challenge is to continue to develop a systems-thinking lens by analyzing and building games in G*M. Youths will consider how games are systems, and they will analyze those systems in terms of their components, the behaviors of those components, and most important, the interconnections that they make. Youths will begin to design games in G*M, and then they will review and discuss different top-down game spaces and model one chosen space in G*M.

DESIGN CHALLENGE 3: DESIGNING PLATFORM GAMES

Total time: 185 minutes

The goal of this challenge is to continue to develop facility with game-design tools and to consider games in terms of their properties as systems. In this challenge, youths will add to their current conceptualization of systems by considering how the structure of a system is related to its function. By altering specific components and examining the impact of the changes on the system's overall function, youths will continue to investigate the ways that interconnections among components work to build a system. Youths will be introduced within G*M to a style of game known as a "platform" or "side-scroller," which they will use to create a world that another person can explore through playing the game. Throughout the activity, youths should be encouraged to describe their designs in terms of the components that they have chosen, the behaviors of the components that they specified, how those behaviors interconnected, and especially, how those interconnections affected the overall way that their game functions. They will complete this activity by modeling (and fixing) a different system, called the "broken lunchroom."

DESIGN CHALLENGE 4: BALANCING THE GAME

Total time: 135 minutes

The goal of this challenge is for youths to better understand and practice with the key systems thinking idea of interconnections (that is, the components within a system relate or are connected to other components in specific ways that determine how a system functions or the kinds of goals that it can meet). In game design, this is best expressed through the idea of balancing a game, which means making sure that the level of challenge in the game is not too hard or too easy, and that the components are all working well together to express the idea of the game. First, in designing a game, youths will investigate the relationship between enemy sprite parameters and the level of challenge in a game. Through modification of the speed, health, and damage parameters of avatar and enemy sprites, they will discover ways of balancing game play so that the game is neither too difficult nor too easy. Then they will playtest and refine their games.

DESIGN CHALLENGE 5: PATTERNS AND MOVEMENT

Total time: 130 minutes

This challenge creates an opportunity for youths to experiment directly with the interconnections that arise between two specific components: enemy sprites and block sprites. Youths will practice creating different kinds of movement and mechanics by adjusting enemy sprite parameters (such as movement style, start direction, and turn direction). They will be encouraged to consider how the qualities of the game space influence and determine the kinds of possible movement. First, youths will create games with a design goal of including complex patterns of enemy movement, in order to explore the concept that movement is a system defined by a number of different component variables: speed, start direction, turn direction, patrolling, and block placement. Next, they will playtest and refine their games and then reflect on how components of their system are interconnected.

DESIGN CHALLENGE 6: MODELING A PREDATOR-PREY SYSTEM

Total time: 125 minutes

The final challenge of the module will involve modeling a complex system, both on paper and in a game. Youths will explore a predator-prey system and learn about how it works—what its components are, how they interconnect, and how they ultimately shape the overall functioning of the system. If desired, the group also can begin to talk about how a predator-prey system stays in balance through a kind of feedback called balancing feedback. Youths are asked to analyze the real-world system of a predator-prey relationship and to model these systems by making games in G*M.

DESIGN CHALLENGE 1 INTRODUCTION TO GAMES AND GAME DESIGN

Total time: 255 minutes

OVERVIEW

The goal of the first challenge is to introduce youths to key concepts and vocabulary related to games and game design through playing and analyzing digital and non-digital games, as well as through classroom discussions. Specifically, youths will start to think about games as systems that are made up of components, each with its own behavior, which interconnect in order to form the overall way that the system functions.

PRODUCT

Youths will create a list of components that make up a game, develop criteria for evaluating what makes a game "good," and create a playable board game.

TARGETED SYSTEMS THINKING CONCEPTS

In this challenge, youths will be introduced to what a system is, as well as the idea that a game is a kind of system. This will involve identifying a system and defining what systems are. Then they will begin to think about what makes a system function by identifying components of that game, identifying the behaviors of those components, and finally, analyzing how the behaviors of those components interconnect to support the system's realization of its goal.

PARTS

PART 1: WHAT IS A GAME? WHAT MAKES A GAME GOOD?

The goal of Part 1 is for youths to think about a game as a dynamic system that changes through player actions. This will be accomplished first by asking them to play a non-digital game and then think about the game as a system, identifying its components and their behaviors and interconnections. Part 1 culminates in the creation of a shared list of the key components of games, and specifically how these components interconnect to make a good game.

Total time: 35 minutes

PART 2: COLLABORATIVE BOARD GAME DESIGN

Youths will have the opportunity to participate in collaborative game design. Working in groups, they will design, play, and revise a board game using the U-Build Sorry! kit or by an alternative found-object game design activity.

Total time: 155 minutes

PART 3: GETTING FAMILIAR WITH GAMESTAR MECHANIC

Youths will start playing Gamestar Mechanic (G*M). Part 3 will end with them coming up with their own game ideas and sharing them with the whole group.

Total time: 90 minutes

KEY DEFINITIONS

Identifying a system. Specifically, a *system* is a collection of two or more components and processes that interconnect to function as a whole. Speed and comfort in a car for example are created by the interactions of the car's parts and thus are "greater than the sum" of all separate parts of the car. The way a system works is not the result of a single part but is produced by the interaction among the components and/or individual agents within it. A key way to differentiate things that are systems from things that aren't is to consider whether the overall way something works in the world will change if you remove one part of it.

Identify the way a system is functioning. The *function* of a system describes the overall behavior of the system—what it is doing or where it's going over time. A system's function might emerge naturally based on interconnections among components, or it might be the result of an intentional design (in which case, we might also refer to the function of a system as its *goal*). Regardless, the function of a system is the result of the dynamics that occur among components' interconnected behaviors.

Distinguishing the goal of a system. The *goal* of the system is what it was intentionally designed to do. Sometimes this might be the same as the functioning of the system … other times the goal and the function are not aligned.

Identifying components. *Components* are the parts of a system that contribute to its functioning. Without being able to effectively identify the parts of a system, it's hard to understand how a system is actually working and how it might be changed.

Identifying behaviors. *Behaviors* are the specific actions or roles that a component of a system displays under various conditions. Being able to identify behaviors becomes important when we change systems, as often a component will look the same after the change, but its behavior will be different.

Identifying interconnections. *Interconnections* are the different ways that a system's parts, or components, interact with each other through their behaviors and, through those interactions, change the behaviors of other components.

COMMON CORE STATE STANDARDS COVERED—ENGLISH LANGUAGE ARTS	NEXT GENERATION SCIENCE STANDARDS
• R.6–12.7	• 3–5-ETS1–1
• RI.7.9	• 3–5-ETS1–2
• W.6–8.3	• 3–5-ETS1–3
• RST.6–8.3	• MS-ETS1–2
• RST.6–8.7	• MS-ETS1–4
• RST.6–8.9	
• SL.6–12.4	
• SL.7.5	

MATERIALS OVERVIEW

- Materials for a non-digital game to play (e.g., MP3 player/boom box and chairs for playing Musical Chairs)
- Chart paper or writing board for brainstorming and saving group notes
- U-Build Sorry! game design kit (one for every group of four youths is ideal)
- Pencils
- Projector or way to display handouts to entire class
- Computers with a high-speed Internet connection (one per person is ideal)
- A timer
- A class list where you can write down each person's username and password.

HANDOUTS

- "Building Your Own Game"
- "Making Predictions"
- "Reflecting and Revising"
- "Model of a System"
- "What Makes a Good Game?"

OVERALL DESIGN CHALLENGE PREPARATION

- Select a non-digital game to play in class for Part 1
- Acquire four sets of the U-Build Sorry! kit for Part 2
- Make sure to set G*M usernames and passwords for your youths for Part 3

PART 1: WHAT IS A GAME? WHAT MAKES A GAME GOOD?

The goal of Part 1 is for youths to start to think about a game as a kind of system. This will be accomplished first by asking them to play a non-digital game and then think about what allowed each player to meet the game's goal by analyzing its components and their behaviors and interconnections. Part 1 culminates in the creation of a shared list of criteria for components of games and, specifically, how these components interconnect in order to make a good game.

Time: 35 minutes

STUFF TO HAVE HANDY

- Materials for a non-digital game to play (e.g., MP3 player/boombox and chairs for playing Musical Chairs)
- Chart paper or writing board for brainstorming and saving group notes

HANDOUTS

- "Model of a System"
- "What Makes a Good Game?"

PLAY: PLAY A GAME—15 MINUTES

The goal of this activity is to create a shared game play experience for the entire group that can be used to analyze how the game works—how the system accomplishes its goal.

1. Have youths play a non-digital game to start—something simple that your class is already familiar with. The selected game can be a card game, board game, physical game, or social game, though it should be a quick one. Depending on the size of the class, you may decide to split the youths into smaller groups so that each group is playing a game like Rock-Paper-Scissors, or choose a game that the entire class can play as one group, such as Musical Chairs or Red Light, Green Light.

2. Before playing the game, review the rules. It is important that everyone agrees upon the rules of the game before playing. It can be useful to write them on chart paper or the board so that the rules are clearly displayed if needed.

3. Play the game!

RESEARCH: WHAT MAKES A GAME, AND WHAT MAKES A GAME GOOD?—20 MINUTES

After playing the game, begin a discussion with your group about the game they just played and ask them to think about how the game worked. In this discussion, you are going to want to introduce some of the key systems thinking vocabulary that the youths will be using for the rest of the module. It is best to introduce this vocabulary to frame their contributions, rather than immediately giving (and defining) these new terms.

1. Ask youths to reflect on the game by framing aspects of the game that you want them to focus on. Throughout, introduce the key systems thinking vocabulary as it naturally emerges from the participants' discussion of the game. The following questions can be used to facilitate the discussion (answers that are offered are given in terms of the game Musical Chairs; in other cases, answers will vary depending on the game being played):

- What was the goal of the game? (*To make sure that you have a chair to sit in when the music turns off; the ultimate goal is to be the last one sitting.*)

- Was the goal of the game actually seen in the function of the game. In other words, did the game work the way it was supposed to? (*The game ended when there was just one chair and one player sitting in it.*)

- What do we need in order to play the game (what are the components of the game)? (*Chairs, people, music, space to move.*)

- What are these materials for (what behavior does each component have)? (*Chairs are for sitting on; there has to be one fewer chair than the number of persons playing. Music tells you when to go and when to stop—(and it will be turned on or off). Rules tell you what to do when the music stops; sit down on a chair—and do it quickly!*)

- How do these aspects of the game work together (how do the behaviors of the components interconnect)? (*The chairs and the people interact because the people need to sit down, but chairs being present or absent affect whether the people can actually sit down on them. The music interacts with the people, because when the music is on, people move, and when the music is off, people sit down.*)

2. Once the youths have come to a shared understanding of how the game worked, give each student a copy of the "Model of a System" handout or project it for everyone to see. Discuss how the words and ideas they came up with relate to the key ideas identified here.

3. Once you finish discussing elements of a game, ask youths to come up with a list of things that make a good game. Encourage them to think about components that can apply to all games, not just to video games. It might help to brainstorm about a range of games that youths have experienced to facilitate this step. Note any key words, concepts, or ideas on the board that are related to what makes a good game.

4. Once the youths have come up with a set of key words through the whole group discussion, give each person a copy of the "What Makes a Good Game?" worksheet or project it in the class for everyone to see. Discuss how the words and ideas they came up with relate to the key ideas and elements identified here.

DESIGN CHALLENGE 1, PART 1:

MODEL OF A SYSTEM

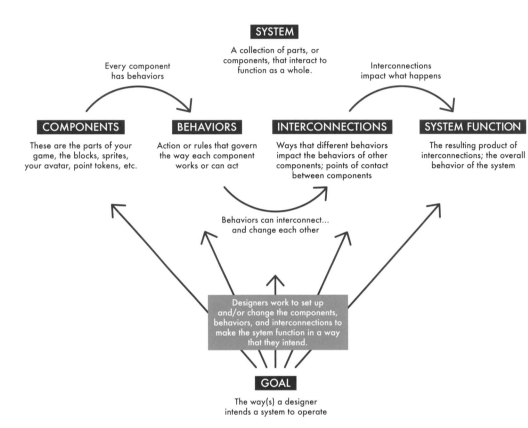

SYSTEM
A collection of parts, or components, that interact to function as a whole.

Every component has behaviors

Interconnections impact what happens

COMPONENTS
These are the parts of your game, the blocks, sprites, your avatar, point tokens, etc.

BEHAVIORS
Action or rules that govern the way each component works or can act

INTERCONNECTIONS
Ways that different behaviors impact the behaviors of other components; points of contact between components

SYSTEM FUNCTION
The resulting product of interconnections; the overall behavior of the system

Behaviors can interconnect... and change each other

Designers work to set up and/or change the components, behaviors, and interconnections to make the sytem function in a way that they intend.

GOAL
The way(s) a designer intends a system to operate

DESIGN CHALLENGE 1, PART 1:

WHAT MAKES A GOOD GAME?

1. Simple Rules.

2. Engaging Gameplay.

3. Has a Goal or a Win/Loss Condition.

4. Choice & Strategy.

5. Conflict.

6. Simple Core Mechanic.

7. Clear Feedback.

8. Challenging.

9. Fair.

10. Expresses an Idea.

WHAT MAKES A GOOD GAME?

1. **Simple Rules.**
   Your game has clear and concise game rules that can be repeated, are shared by all players, and explain what can and cannot be done in the game. Simple rules are easy to understand and can be learned by playing the game.

2. **Engaging Gameplay.**
   This can mean your game is "fun" or "challenging" or "interesting," for example.

3. **Has a Goal or a Win/Loss Condition.**
   Your game has a goal the player is trying to reach to win the game. The goal determines when a player has won or lost the game. A game goal might be collecting a certain number of points, or getting through a maze before time runs out.

4. **Choice & Strategy.**
   Your game should give a player choices that affect the outcome of the game. Allowing for different sets of decisions to be made each time the game is played.

5. **Conflict.**
   Your game should give the player an obstacle or challenge to overcome, creating "conflict." The conflict might be in trying to keep your avatar alive or in capturing a certain amount of territory.

6. **Simple Core Mechanic.**
   Your game should use a simple core mechanic or play pattern that allows the player to meet the game goal. A core mechanic might be collecting points, jumping across platforms, shooting aliens, or running through a maze.

7. **Clear Feedback.**
   Your game should give the player feedback on how well they are doing toward meeting the game goal. Feedback might mean adding a score counter to your game to show how many points have been collected, or a timer that shows how much time the player is taking.

8. **Challenging.**
   Your game should be challenging, neither too hard nor too easy. It should challenge your player to develop mastery over the core mechanic to win. Before you let a player play your game you need to show that it can be beat.

9. **Fair.**
   Game should provide an equal chance for each player to win.

10. **Expresses an Idea.**
    Your game should express an idea or logic in its design. This idea defines the game as an integrated system rather than a set of random parts, which includes the visual design.

PART 2: COLLABORATIVE GAME DESIGN: USING BOARD GAMES TO PRACTICE ITERATING AND IMPROVING DESIGNS

The goal of Part 2 is to give youths an opportunity to engage in collaborative game design by having them design, play, and revise a board game that their peers will play and give them feedback on. In completing this activity, youths will have the opportunity to design a multiplayer board game and think about how the particular decisions that they make affect the goal of the game and how changing particular components of the game may change the behavior of other components, and ultimately, the entire game experience. During this activity, youths will be responsible for creating a game that others will set up and play in small teams. Starting with a non-digital game design assignment will give youths a concrete jumping-off point for observing a game system at work.

Time: 155 minutes

STUFF TO HAVE HANDY

- U-Build Sorry! game design kit (one for every group of four youths is ideal)
- Pencils
- Chart paper or writing board
- Projector or way to display handouts to entire class

HANDOUTS

- "Building Your Own Game"
- "Making Predictions"
- "Reflecting and Revising"

VOICES FROM THE FIELD

Working [first] on tactile projects, like U-build, improved the students' participation in the challenges ... [before] moving into the virtual world.

—TRAVIS POWELL, OREGON WRITING PROJECT

RESEARCH: GETTING READY FOR DESIGN—10 MINUTES

Introduce the U-build activity as an opportunity to explore game design collectively, and then collaborate to design a game as a group. You will want to make sure that everyone understands the goal of the activity, as well as how to use the U-Build Sorry! game design kit.

1. Show the U-Build Sorry! game design kit to the group. Youths are going to want to think about all of the components of the game design kit that are available to them as they design a game of their own. Make sure that youths are aware of all of the components of the game design kit, and make sure that they have a sense of what those components might be used for. It is important to emphasize that there is *no one right way* to build a game using these pieces. The following questions and prompts can be used to facilitate the discussion:

- Let's take a look at the board, which we can also call the *game space*. What are the components of the board, and what might the behavior of those components be? (*Some possible answers: the board has different colors, these different colors are each on one corner of the board—the behavior of these colors might relate to being starting points for particular colors, or indications of extra power for particular colors. There's also some color-specific shading on each corner, which might give information about what direction to move. There are spaces to put in blocks, which might serve to direct the movement of players.*)

- Let's take a look at the pieces that come with the game—these are also components of the game. What could they do in a game that you create? (*Some possible answers: there are game pieces that come in four colors and two sizes; that might mean that four people can play; the size might indicate different kinds of power or value; there are white blocks and colored blocks, which might help to direct action of the pieces around the board; maybe the colors would be specifically related to the color pieces; there's a grabber that could*

be used to save players if they get trapped in other people's spots; there are two different kinds of dice, etc.)

- What are some possible rules that the game might have? How would those rules relate to (or affect) the components? *(The goal here is for youths to start to appreciate that rules often actually govern the behavior of the components or describe their interconnections.)*

2. Instruct youths that they will be working in teams (we suggest groups of three to four) with a goal of creating two versions or iterations of a game. This will involve keeping close track of time and also taking careful notes about initial design decisions, outcomes, proposed changes, and their results.

3. Pass out the "Building Your Own Game" worksheet, and explain that its purpose is to support their documentation of the phases of their game design.

CREATE, PLAY, AND ITERATE: COLLABORATIVE GAME DESIGN—85 MINUTES

Now is the chance for youths to actually begin to design. There are two handouts that will guide this process: "Building Your Own Game" and "Making Predictions." Be sure to help youths keep track of time, as it is easy to get so caught up in designing and playing that there won't be time to do a second round of designing and playing—and the contrast between the first and the second round is really important in encouraging youths to start thinking about how components of games interconnect to support the ultimate game experience (the goal). Youths will be working in groups for the entire time; the following is a suggested breakdown of the time and what they should be doing at each phase.

The overall time breakdown for this activity, outlined in the steps listed next, is as follows:

- Initial Design Period—30 minutes

- First Playtest Period—10 minutes

- First Iteration Period—10 minutes

- Second Playtest Period—15 minutes

- Finalizing the Design—20 minutes

1. It might be helpful for youths to write up the particular timing breakdown during the days that this activity is running so that they can keep track of time.

2. For the sake of accountability, you might want to assign roles to youths in each group. These roles can help to distribute responsibility for particular tasks, help keep track of time and where the group is in the design cycle, and ensure that everyone has a way to participate. We suggest the following roles, but of course, any roles that you think would be productive or are already in use with your youths will be useful. If you assign roles, you might want the entire group to work collectively on the "Building Your Own Game," "Making Predictions," and "Reflecting on Your Game" worksheets.

- **Note taker:** This person is responsible for recording initial plans and iterations of designs. (These will be noted on the "Building Your Own Game" handout.)

- **Prediction manager:** This person is responsible for keeping the group on task and making sure that the group is anticipating what sort of impact different design decisions will have on the game play. (This will be noted on the "Making Predictions" handout.)

- **Materials manager:** This person is in charge of accounting for all the components in the game and ensuring that all the components have behaviors associated with them (or, if the group chooses not to use some components, this person will be sure that the oversight was intentional).

- **Reflection master:** This person is in charge of recording what happens during game play, what was intended, and what was not anticipated in terms of how the game actually went when it was played. (These will be noted on the "Reflecting and Revising" handout.)

MOD THIS ACTIVITY: FOUND OBJECT GAME DESIGN

If you can't find or don't have access to the U-Build Sorry! game design kit, it's possible to do a version of this activity that's based on "found objects"— items found around the game design room. These can include pencils, balls, poker chips, maps or globes, balloons, popsicle sticks, toothpicks, magazines . . . the possibilities are limited only by your or the youths' imaginations (although it's best to gather materials ahead of time and make sure that you have a diverse selection!).

In this mod, explain to the group that they will be using found objects to create a never-before-seen game that utilizes these objects and has a clear set of rules of play. Break the larger group into teams, and then have a representative from each team select a limited number of items from a pile of found objects. Engage in selection "rounds," allowing each team to pick only 1–2 items at a time so that all teams have the chance at the most popular items, but teams should end up with 10–12 items. Once the teams have their objects, review the goal of the activity and solicit questions to make sure everyone understands.

The overall structure and timing for the activity shouldn't have to change very much from the original U-Build Sorry! exercise—plan to engage in the same iterative design cycle, make slight modifications to the handouts, and engage in the discussion and reflection process just as you would if you were using the U-Build Sorry! kit. The one thing to pay particular attention to is making comparisons effectively of what might be very different game designs across groups. In the discussion, point out broad trends that speak to the particular ideas around systems thinking and design that emerge from that activity.

---

3. Using the "Building Your Own Game" handout to guide their discussion, ask youths to begin their first design, letting them know that they'll have about a half hour to work on it. For your reference, they will be addressing the following issues:

- What does the board look like (game space)?

- What components are you using? What can they do? What kinds of actions or mechanics might they allow for a player?

- How do you play your game (what are the rules)?

4. After about 30 minutes, remind youths that it is time to begin their first play test of their game. Have them start with forecasting about their game with the "Making Predictions" worksheet, and then play their game, recording the accuracy of their predictions and what surprised them. Let them know that they have about 10 minutes to playtest.

5. Using the "Reflecting and Revising" worksheet, have youths reflect on what happened when they played their game and decide what sorts of changes they want to make to it during the first iteration period. This period should last about 10 minutes.

6. As they finish the second iteration of their game, and before the second playtest period, have each group make predictions about their game using the "Making Predictions" worksheet. As they engage in the second playtest period, they should record the accuracy of their predictions and what surprised them. The second

playtest period should last about 15 minutes. Remind them that this is their last playtest before they finalize their design and have another team play it.

7. Using the "Reflecting and Revising" worksheet, have youths reflect on their second draft game.

8. Let the group know that now they should work for the next 20 minutes on the final design of their game, the one that will be played by another group. Returning to the "Building Your Own Game" worksheet, support youths in creating the final draft of their game using the same questions, but this time also recording what is *different* from their first draft. Encourage them to make sure that what they write down will be understandable by another team that will be playing their game.

9. After the allotted time, have youths complete what they're doing and finalize their game design.

SHARE: TEAM GAME SWAP—45 MINUTES

Now that the teams have gone through multiple cycles of design and iteration on their games, it's time for them to allow other groups to play so they can get external feedback on what the play experience is like. The game swap creates an authentic context for their creations to be tested by others, and also gives them the opportunity to make sure that they have a clear sense of their own designs. Finally, it creates an opportunity for feedback on their final designs.

1. Put pairs of teams together, letting them know that they will be using their "Building Your Own Game" handout as means of sharing the rules of their game with the other team. Make sure that each team leaves a member behind with the game to observe game play and help clarify the rules during the swap session. Have each team spend about 5 minutes before playing, to make sure that they understand how the game works.

2. Once teams are clear on the rules, let the game play begin! Allow about 20 minutes for game play, with the opportunity for a second round if time allows. Encourage players to think about what sort of feedback they want to share.

3. After the game play period ends, have the pairs of teams come together to give each other warm and cool feedback on their designs (see section on "Designing a Supportive Learning Environment" in the Introduction, [pages 13–15], for feedback tips), sharing what they thought worked well, what they thought could be improved, and any additional thoughts they might have. Have each team spend about 10 minutes doing this, and then have the teams switch, with one giving feedback and the other listening.

REFLECT: THE RELATIONSHIP(S) AMONG COMPONENTS, BEHAVIORS, AND GOALS — 15 MINUTES

Once youths complete their games, facilitate a whole-group discussion to help them reflect on their game designs. (Note that this is something that you could actually do twice—once in the middle of the game design session and once at the end.) The purpose of the discussion is to help youths to think about the creation of goals, the use of game space, and the interaction between game components.

The following questions can be used to facilitate the discussion.

DESIGN-BASED THINKING

- What was the goal of your game? What decisions did you make in designing your game that were related to the goal?

- Did the overall function of your game match the goal? Why or why not?

- What was one thing you changed from game 1 to game 2? What difference did that decision make in terms of the overall functioning of your game? How do you know?

- What was one thing that made your game really good? (Students might reference the list of criteria listed in part 1 for this answer.)

- Were there any design decisions that you made that ended up making your game bad or not fun? Why?

- When designing a game, what is the point of going through several rounds of design?

- What role did the testing and feedback activity play in your design?

SYSTEMS THINKING

- Choose two components (e.g., avatars, dice, the gripper), and explain how they interact in your game. Is there another component in your game that doesn't interact with those two components?

- Was your game challenging? What made it challenging? What is one thing you could change to make it more challenging?

- What change could you make to your game (or that you did make to your game) that changed the overall game-play experience?

- What change could you make to your game (or that you did make to your game) that didn't change the overall game-play experience?

WHAT TO EXPECT

Some youths may come to you already understanding some aspects of design-based or systems thinking concepts, while others will be total novices to these ideas. The following chart was designed to give you an overall sense of the ways these two groups—novices and experts—might behave and react during this activity. Note that progressing from novice to expert is an ongoing process, and it's possible that a youth will not completely fit into the "novice" or "expert" classification. You might look for evidence of youths' understanding both on the "Reflecting and Revising" handout that they complete and in the whole-group discussion.

Assessing Youths' Systems Thinking

	Novice	Expert
Design-based thinking concepts	• Does not systematically change one element at a time to see the larger effects on game play • Doesn't know how to "test" a change in order to determine its impact • Thinks about each component of the game individually, rather than considering its interactions with other components	• Changes one component of the game at a time to test its effect on the game as a whole • Plays a game through to the end to determine the effect of particular design decisions • In designing, considers interactions among components and how they affect game play
Systems thinking concepts	• Thinks causally (rather than interactively) about components in the game (e.g., if you want the game to be harder, add a time limit) • Believes that changing the overall game play requires large changes in the behavior of the game components • Doesn't understand how components of the system interact to produce a specific game-play experience	• Sees the overall game play experience (the system) as being based on interactions among components (e.g., changing one component changes the game only to the extent that it affects the behaviors of other elements) • Recognizes that sometimes a small change to a component can make a significant impact on the overall behavior of the system (game-play experience) • Has a sense of how the components of the system interact and affect one another

DESIGN CHALLENGE 1, PART 2

BUILDING YOUR OWN GAME

This handout is designed to help you keep track of the different games that you design, and specifically, to make sure that you have included all the components that are available in your game. (If you don't want to include everything, that's okay—but make sure that there is a good reason not to include them!) The first column of the table is for the first draft of your game; the second column is for the second draft. The table is organized this way so that you can easily see what you have *changed* from design 1 to design 2, so that you can think about how particular changes that your group made affected how the game actually went.

First Draft	Second Draft
Game Space (Board) What does the board look like? Do specific areas of the game space act in particular ways?	**Game Space (Board)** What does the board look like? Do specific areas of the game space act in particular ways? How is it different from the first draft?
Components What components are you using? What can they do?	**Components** What components are you using? What can they do? How is this different from your first draft?
Rules How do you play your game?	**Rules** How do you play your game? How is this different from your first draft?

DESIGN CHALLENGE 1, PART 2

MAKING PREDICTIONS

Before you play your game ...

Think about one element of your game (i.e., blocks, avatars, dice, the gripper, rules, or goals). Describe how you think that element is going to affect your game play.

Now play your game with your group!

What was accurate about your prediction?

What happened that surprised you?

DESIGN CHALLENGE 1, PART 2

REFLECTING AND REVISING

After you've played your game: Take some time to consider what happened during play and why.

First Draft	Second Draft
What made your game challenging?	What made your game challenging?
How could you change your game to make it more challenging?	How could you change your game to make it more challenging?
What could you change that would make the biggest impact on the functioning of the game?	What could you change that would make the biggest impact on the functioning of the game?
Why would that have such a big impact on the functioning of the game?	Why would that have such a big impact on the functioning of the game?
What could you change that would make the smallest impact on the functioning of the game?	What could you change that would make the smallest impact on the functioning of the game?
Why would that have such a small impact on the functioning of the game?	Why would that have such a small impact on the functioning of the game?

PART 3: GETTING FAMILIAR WITH G*M

The goal of Part 3 is to get youths familiar with G*M by having them ideally play through the four missions in *Episode 1: Journey to Factory 7* of G*M, followed by a discussion on the design process of game designers and how they use different strategies for coming up with game ideas. In addition, youths will come up with their own game ideas and share them with the whole group.

Time: 90 minutes

STUFF TO HAVE HANDY

- Pencils
- Chart paper or writing board
- Computers with a high-speed Internet connection (one computer per child is ideal)
- A timer
- A class list where you can write down each person's username and password

HANDOUTS

- "Model of a System"
- "What Makes a Good Gamestar Minigame?" (p. 48)

PLAY: PLAY G*M—60 MINUTES

Have students navigate online to the Gamestar Mechanic website (**gamestarmechanic .com/log/in/**) to create new accounts.

1. Click on the "Login or Register now!" link at the top of the home page, and then click on "Sign up now!"
2. Fill in the information requested to register. Be sure that you help students to choose usernames and passwords *that they will remember*.

Gamestar Mechanic uses **fun, game-based quests and courses** to help you learn game design and make your own video games!

Get started!

Have an account? **Log In!**

Want more info?

For Teachers

For Parents

Take an Online Course

Privacy policy

Not a Member?

Sign up now!

3. Ask them to share this information with you so that if they forget (and they will!), it will be easy to recover their information.

4. Students will be asked to create a security code by selecting from a number of objects.

5. They will be prompted to select the type of account. Ask students to select "Free Account."

6. Have youths log in and play through *Episode 1: Journey to Factory 7* in G*M.

Youths should work their way through all four missions in the first episode (*Mission 1: Naviron Adventure; Mission 2: Altair Journey;*

Step 1: Create your new account

Already have an account? Click here to log in!

Username:

Password:

Confirm Password:

Birthday: Month ▾ Day ▾ Year ▾ ?

☐ I have read and agree to the Gamestar Mechanic Terms of Service.

Register!

Mission 3: Acheron Gauntlet; and *Mission 4: Kerakuri Mindbender).* These challenges are structured to scaffold the student into the game environment while introducing key ideas about how to build quality games. How quickly youths work through these missions will depend largely on how familiar they are with video games; generally youths who have more experience playing video games go through the missions much more quickly than youths who are relative novices. For youths who cannot complete the missions in an hour, encourage them to continue to play at home or in another space where they have computer access, if they can. Youths who complete the missions in less than an hour can explore some of the offerings in GAME ALLEY, a space where users share their own designed games and critique each other's.

Note that youths cannot publish and share their own games with others until the end of *Episode 5: The Balance Room* (covered here in Design Challenge 5).

RESEARCH AND REFLECT: HOW DOES A GAME DESIGNER CREATE A GAME?—15 MINUTES

1. Begin a whole-group discussion about the games they played in G*M and how they think the game designers created those games. You might share some of these quotes from professional game designers to get the conversation started:

- "I always start by thinking about a story for my game. Then I build the world and create a game that can be played in that world."

- "I love thinking about play patterns, so I always start with a cool game mechanic, like jumping or collecting."

- "Space is my thing—I always design the game space first and then figure out what kind of creatures could play in the space."

- "Sometimes I just start messing around with sprites and see where my ideas go!"

2. Ask youths to imagine where the G*M game designers came up with an idea for the game and what series of steps they might have taken to create it.

3. Using the "Model of a System" handout, ask youths to analyze one of the games that they played in terms of the *goal* of the game, the *components* that were included in the game, how those components *behaved*, and what *interconnections* they observed between the components. For this discussion, it will be important to ensure that everyone has played and is discussing the same game. In addition, you might want to project the game that is being discussed so the whole group can see it.

4. Using the "What Makes a Good Gamestar Minigame?" handout, ask youths to think about how the 10 items were reflected (or not) in the games that they played. This can be completed as a whole class, in small groups, or individually. The goal here is for youths to begin to see the logic and intentionality behind the design of the games that they just played. Encourage the youths to use both images and words.

WHAT TO EXPECT

The previous discussions give youths an opportunity to reflect on game play using a new vocabulary. This will be at least the third application of these terms to a game context, so it is likely that they will become more fluent both with the terms and with the ideas. Pay attention to the ways that youths describe and talk about their game play, particularly with respect to their analysis of these games as systems, to look for this kind of growth.

	Novice	Expert
Design-based thinking concepts	• Does not systematically change one component at a time to see the larger effects on game play • Doesn't know how to "test" a change to determine its impact • Thinks about each component of the game individually, rather than considering its interactions with other components	• Changes one component of the game at a time to test its effect on the game as a whole • Plays a game through to the end to determine the effect of particular design decisions • In designing, considers interactions among components and how they affect game play
Systems thinking concepts	• Thinks causally (rather than interactively) about components in the game (e.g., if you want the game to be harder, add a time limit) • Believes that changing the overall game play requires large changes in the behavior of the game components • Doesn't understand how components of the system interact to produce a specific game-play experience	• Sees the overall game play experience (the system) as being based on interactions among components (e.g., changing one component only changes the game to the extent that it affects the behaviors of other components) • Recognizes that sometimes a small change to a component can make a significant impact on the overall behavior of the system (game-play experience) • Has a sense of how the components of the system interact and affect one another

IMAGINE: GAME IDEA BRAINSTORM—15 MINUTES

1. Set the timer to 5 minutes and challenge youths to come up with five game ideas each. An idea might look something like, "An alien goes on a trip around the galaxy," or "Massive treasure hunt for lost gold," or "Monsters invade an underground cavern in search of magic cookies."

2. Have them write down their ideas on index cards or sticky notes. Once time is up, have the youths post all their cards on the wall.

3. Share ideas as time allows. Keep these cards on the wall for future reference and encourage youths to keep a set of index cards with them so they can work on game ideas throughout the day. These ideas can be posted to a class blog (if you are using one) and can become a valuable class resource for later sessions when youths need a bit of inspiration!

DESIGN CHALLENGE 2
DESIGNING TOP-DOWN GAMES

Total time: 125 minutes

OVERVIEW

The goal of this challenge is to continue to develop a systems thinking lens by analyzing and building games in Gamestar Mechanic (G*M). Youths will consider how the games are systems, and they will analyze those systems in terms of their components, the behaviors of those components, and most important, the interconnections that they make.

PRODUCT

Youths will design "top-down" games in G*M.

TARGETED SYSTEMS THINKING CONCEPTS

In this challenge, youths will continue to think about what makes a system function by analyzing the purpose or goal of the system of a game by identifying components of that game, identifying the behaviors of those components, and finally, examining how the behaviors of those components interconnect to support the system's realization of its goal. In addition, youths will start to build a game (modeled after an existing game), and consider how the components of that game interconnect to support the realization of its goal.

PARTS

PART 1: BECOME A GAMESTAR MECHANIC

In this part, youths will begin to design games in G*M. The goal of this part is twofold: first, to introduce youths to the design tools of the platform, and second, for youths to begin to use the vocabulary of systems to describe and make sense of what they have designed. Specifically, youths should be encouraged to describe their designs in terms of the components that they have chosen, the behaviors of the components that they specified, how those behaviors interconnected, how those interconnections affect the overall functioning of the system, and how the interconnections helped achieve the intended goal.

Time: 65 minutes

PART 2: TOP-DOWN-STYLE GAMES

In this part, youths will have an opportunity to review and discuss different top-down game spaces and model one chosen space in G*M. Youths again will engage in systems thinking practices by identifying the components of a system, creating a diagram or list of those components, and showing how the components relate to each other within the system.

Time: 60 minutes

KEY DEFINITIONS

Identifying a system. Specifically, a *system* is a collection of two or more components and processes that interconnect to function as a whole. Speed and comfort in a car for example are created by the interactions of the car's parts and thus are "greater than the sum" of all separate parts of the car. The way a system works is not the result of a single part but is produced by the interaction among the components and/or individual agents within it. A key way to differentiate things that are systems from things that aren't is to consider whether the overall way something works in the world will change if you remove one part of it.

Identifying the way a system is functioning. The *function* of a system describes the overall behavior of the system—what it is doing or where it's going over time. A system's function might emerge naturally based on interconnections among components, or it might be the result of an intentional design (in which case we might also refer to the function of a system as its goal). Regardless, the function of a system is the result of the dynamics that occur among components' interconnected behaviors.

Distinguishing the goal of a system. The *goal* of the system is what it was intentionally designed to do. Sometimes this might be the same as the function of the system … other times the goal and the function are not aligned.

Identifying components. *Components* are the parts of a system that contribute to its functioning. Without being able to effectively identify the parts of a system, it's hard to understand how a system is actually working and how it might be changed.

Identifying behaviors. *Behaviors* are the specific actions or roles that a component of a system displays under various conditions. Being able to identify behaviors becomes important when we change systems, as often a component will look the same after the change, but its behavior will be different.

Identifying interconnections. *Interconnections* are the different ways that a system's parts, or components, interact with each other through their behaviors and through those interactions change the behaviors of other components.

Make systems visible. When we "make the system visible"—whether modeling a system on the back of a napkin, through a computer simulation, a game, a picture, a diagram, a set of mathematical computations, or a story—we can use these representations to communicate about how things work. At their best, good pictures of systems help both the creator and the reader or audience to understand not only the parts of the system (the components) but also how those components work together to produce a whole.

COMMON CORE STATE STANDARDS COVERED—ENGLISH LANGUAGE ARTS	NEXT GENERATION SCIENCE STANDARDS
• W.6–8.3	• 3–5-ETS1–1
• RST.6–8.3	• 3–5-ETS1–2
• RST.6–8.7	• 3–5-ETS1–3
• RST.6–8.9	• MS-ETS1–2
• SL.6–12.4	• MS-ETS1–4
• SL.7.5	

MATERIALS OVERVIEW

- Digital projector

HANDOUTS

- "Screen Shot of Workshop"
- "Model of a System"
- "Top-Down Video Game Examples"

OVERALL CHALLENGE PREPARATION

- Within G*M, make sure that you, as the teacher/facilitator, play through *Episode 2: Elevator Emergency*.

- Within G*M, make sure that you go to the Workshop area and design your own game so that you can become familiar with three design components: the Level Editor, Sprite Inventory, and Tools.

PART 1: BECOME A GAMESTAR MECHANIC

In this part, youths will begin to design games in G*M. The goal of this part is twofold: first, to introduce youths to the design tools in the game; and second, for youths to begin to use the *vocabulary of systems* to describe and make sense of what they have designed. Specifically, youths should be encouraged to describe their designs in terms of the components that they have chosen, the behaviors of the components that they specified, how those behaviors interconnected, how those interconnections affected the overall functioning of the system, and how the interconnections helped achieve the goal of the game.

Time: 65 minutes

STUFF TO HAVE HANDY

- Digital projector

HANDOUTS

- "Screen Shot of Workshop"
- "Model of a System" completed in Design Challenge 1

VOICES FROM THE FIELD

Top-down, platform, and U-Build … oh my!?! After another full day teaching G*M, I could feel the excitement and frustration that game designers must experience. I was very excited about seeing the designs come to life. I watched youths test avatars and enemies, change their power balance, and import them into the game grid. I also watched youths work on developing the ultimate game field for their sprites to take advantage of.

—DEIDRA FLOYD, CENTRAL TEXAS WRITING PROJECT

PLAY: PLAY G*M—20 MINUTES

Ideally, youths should have completed four missions in *Episode 1: Journey to Factory 7* by the end of Design Challenge 1. In Design Challenge 2, youths can start playing *Episode 2: Elevator Emergency*, which comprises two missions. *Episode 2* begins with the youth (represented in the comic by the male or female avatar "Madison," who wants to become a Gamestar Mechanic) being stuck in an elevator. The youth must fix the system to make it work again. Once each youth has gone through the two missions, the comic will show their avatar being accepted to the Gamestar Mechanic school.

If youths finish their missions early, you can have them go to the Workshop to design a game until their peers have caught up, or have them go to Game Alley, where they can play published games. Alternatively, it is OK if youths move to *Episode 3: Samson's League of Mechanics* after finishing the two missions in *Episode 2*.

RESEARCH: PREPARING FOR DESIGN—10 MINUTES

Before youths begin to design, you'll want to give them a brief overview of how the tools work. This works best if you ask youths to turn off their monitors or close their laptops and project your computer for the whole group to follow the procedure together as you demonstrate it.

1. Introduce youths to the following (see the "Screenshot of Workshop"):

    a. Tools: Give an overview of the tools available in the editor:

    - Edit/Play button
    - Level Design tool
    - Erase tool
    - Move tool
    - Add a Level button
    - Game Title
    - Save button
    - Wrench tool

    The wrench tool will be used in Design Challenge 3.

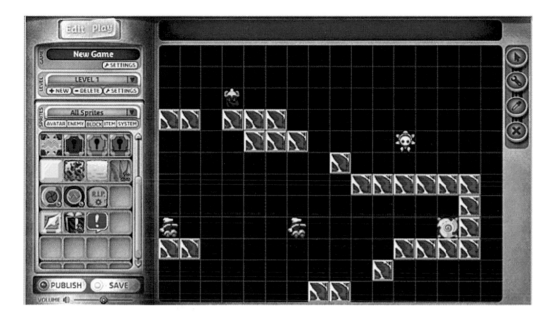

b. LEVEL EDITOR: Click on the Level Design tool and go over the five different components that make up a game space:

- *Gravity**—whether the player falls down or stays stable

- *Edge conditions*—whether and where the game space is bounded or unbounded.

- *Scrolling*—a single screen or multiple screens

- *Background*—the picture/image that appears in the background of the game

- *Soundtrack*—optional music that can be included

c. Sprite Inventory: Introduce the five different kinds of sprites:

- *Avatar*—the representation of the player

- *Enemy*—bad guys who can damage you

- *Block*—cubes that divide the game space into different areas

---

* Note that for this first activity, youths will be asked to design top-down games, which do *not* include gravity.

- *Item*—functional and nonfunctional components that can be added to the game

- *System*—elements that define certain goal conditions for the game, like a timer, point counter, or frag counter

2. After youths understand what the tools are and how they work, prepare them to start thinking about the game that they are planning to design. You might want to remind them of the conversations that you had in Design Challenge 1 about the various inspirations that game designers have for the games that they create. If you wrote down a list of inspirations, you might want to show it again. If not, it's a good idea to do a little collective brainstorming before youths begin to design.

3. Encourage youths to make a plan for what they want their game to be like before they get involved with the tools. The plan can always change, but it's often helpful for youths to be at least somewhat intentional about their design, as the many tools and choices can easily become overwhelming. Alternatively, you can ask the entire group to design under a set of constraints that might include the following:

- Make a game that uses at least 1 sprite from each category (Avatar, Enemy, Items, Blocks, and System), but no more than 5 from a single category, except for blocks.

- Make a game without enemies that is still challenging.

- Make a game that does not use any special items (health pack, power-ups, blaster, etc.) or special blocks (keys, doors, glass blocks, etc.).

- Make a game using the following sprites: 1 avatar, 1 type of enemy, colored blocks only, points, and a goal block.

CREATE: DESIGN A GAME IN G*M—20 MINUTES

Once youths have a plan, they implement it by using the following process, which is designed to help them work mindfully:

1. Ask youths to get into pairs or small groups and discuss their game ideas. This can be done very quickly: many youths will still be unsure what their games will look like because they haven't had a chance to play with the tools yet.

2. Once youths are clear on their designs, ask them to log in to their accounts in G*M (gamestarmechanic.com). Then instruct them to click on "Workshop" and scroll down and click on "Make a new game!"

3. Give youths about 20 minutes to design their games in G*M. **Note:** Encourage them to save their game frequently!

SHARE AND REFLECT: GAMES AND THE SYSTEMS THEY REPRESENT—15 MINUTES

Once youths complete their games (or at least have a draft), return to the "Model of a System" worksheet from Design Challenge 1. Ask youths to take 5 minutes individually to map the game that they designed onto the model, identifying the components, behaviors, interconnections, and overall goal of the game.

Ask for volunteers or select specific youths who have designed very different games to show their game quickly to the entire group. Ask the whole group to reflect on the following questions for each example:

- What was the goal of the game?

- Did the game's function match the designer's goal?

- What are the components of the game?

- What behaviors does each component have?

- How do the behaviors of the components interconnect and impact each other?

WHAT TO EXPECT

These questions are identical to the questions that were discussed in Design Challenge 1. You might note some development in youths' thinking as they continue to apply the same vocabulary and big ideas across multiple games.

Novice	Expert
• Thinks causally (rather than interactively) about elements in the game (e.g., if you want the game to be harder, add a time limit) • Believes that changing the overall game play requires large changes in the behavior of the game elements • Doesn't understand how elements of the system interact to produce a specific game-play experience	• Sees the overall game-play experience (the system) as being based on interactions among elements (e.g., changing one element changes the game only to the extent that it affects the behaviors of other elements) • Recognizes that sometimes a small change to an element can make a significant impact on the overall behavior of the system (game-play experience) • Has a sense of how the elements of the system interact and affect one another

DESIGN CHALLENGE 2, PART 1

SCREENSHOT OF WORKSHOP

Level Editor allows you to change:
- perspective
- scrolling
- edge bounding
- background
- music

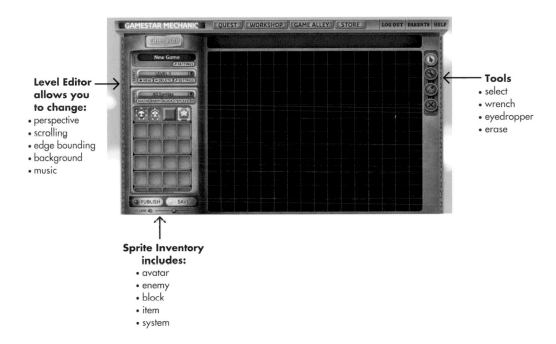

Tools
- select
- wrench
- eyedropper
- erase

Sprite Inventory includes:
- avatar
- enemy
- block
- item
- system

PART 2: DESIGNING TOP-DOWN GAMES

In this part, youths will have an opportunity to review and discuss different top-down game spaces and model the space of their choice in G*M. Youths again will identify the components of a system, create a diagram or list of those components, and show how the components relate to each other within the system.

Time: 60 minutes

STUFF TO HAVE HANDY

- Digital projector

HANDOUTS

- "Model of a System" (from Design Challenge 1)
- "Top-Down Video Game Examples"

RESEARCH—WHAT IS A TOP-DOWN GAME?—20 MINUTES

Take a few moments to review some examples of top-down games available on the market today. Most youths will be familiar with at least some of these games, but they won't have thought about what components and behaviors set them apart from other game formats.

1. Display (and if possible, play) a top-down game (not one from G*M), using the projector. See "Top-Down Video Game Examples" or explore the top-down video games category available on Wikipedia. Ask youths to help you identify the components that make up the space of the top-down game. For example, in Pac-Man, there is a dark background broken into sections by light walls. Ask youths if these components are meant to represent something else that might appear in the real world. If so, help youths think about how the game designer decided to represent them in the game. Point out that sprites like Pac-Man and the ghosts can be modeled in G*M. The sprite Pac-Man needs to collect points, similar to the ones available in the G*M inventory.

2. Ask youths to help you identify the behaviors of the components of the top-down game, and then talk about any interconnections that they can identify among the components' behaviors.

3. Do this same task with at least one other top-down game, and then ask youths to think about what these games have in common ... and how they differ from other games that they might play. Specifically, we want youths to notice that these top-down games are played from a bird's-eye view and don't include any model for gravity.

CREATE: MODEL A TOP-DOWN GAME — 30 MINUTES

Challenge youths to create a game in G*M that imitates the game or game space that they just analyzed. Remind them to think about how the sprites can be used to represent the different components of the space that they identified. It may be helpful to reiterate to youths that top-down style games do not use gravity. You might want to direct youths to either talk in pairs or give a brief sketch of the game that they plan to model. When youths are ready to design in G*M, have them return to their computers and begin the activity.

1. For the next activity to work, youths *must* have redeemed a special code within G*M that provides access to the challenges in *Gaming the System*. If this hasn't been done, direct them to follow this link: **gamestarmechanic.com/?activation =GAMINGTHESYSTEM**. They will be prompted to login (if they haven't already). They then click the Redeem button.

2. Have the youths click on the "WORKSHOP" tab and then scroll down to "Challenges and Contests." For this activity, they are looking for the challenge called Top-Down Perspective. Click this to open the challenge.

3. Within the Top-Down Perspective challenge area are four tabs that you will want to review briefly:

   • "Challenge Missions" provides examples of top-down games for youths to play and explore (note that some of these have to be unlocked by completing easier games).

   • "Design Brief" explains the rules and requirements for completing the challenge.

   • "Create an Entry" is the design space where youths can go to create their own games.

   • "Other Entries" is the storage area where their own and others' game entries are housed.

4. Give youths about 20 minutes to design their games in G*M. Encourage them to save their game frequently.

   • You may want to remind them to think about how the sprites can be used to represent the different components of the space. Dirt blocks, for example, can be used to represent a mountain, points can be used to represent gold, etc.

   • Youths might attempt to create multiple levels, so it may be helpful to constrain them to create a game with only one level.

VOICES FROM THE FIELD

As I walked around, I reminded youth that the point of having constraints in this game design session was to focus on the characteristics of each avatar and enemy (i.e., strength, health, and speed) and how the attributes of those components affect the strategies needed to accomplish the goals of the games they are creating.

—TRAVIS POWELL, OREGON WRITING PROJECT

SHARE AND REFLECT: WHERE'S THE SYSTEM IN YOUR GAME?—10 MINUTES

Youths are unlikely to consider systems thinking while designing their games, but of course, they are gaining experience with fundamental systems thinking ideas as they design games for themselves. Specifically, they will begin to observe interactions among components—that is, when they change one component, other components are affected, even if that wasn't part of their original intent. The purpose of this whole-group discussion is to try to help youths give voice to these ideas and, particularly, attach *systems thinking vocabulary* to these experiences.

Gather youths together to share how their game works. **Note:** To guide the reflection, you may find it helpful to encourage youths to talk about how they modeled their game environments. Point it out if they are using any of the terms outlined in the "Model of a System" handout from Design Challenge 1. If they don't use that terminology, take time to match their words to the formal terms used in the "Model of a System" handout (*components, behaviors, interconnections, function,* and *goal*).

1. Have a few individuals explain their models to the whole group by displaying and playing them on the projector.

2. Use the following questions to facilitate discussion:

   • What are the similarities and differences between your game and the game that you modeled?

   • What components are in your game, and what are the qualities and attributes of each component?

   • What are the interconnections between those components?

3. Use the following question stems to help youths reframe how they talk about their games (i.e., to help them focus more on the relationships between components embedded in their game):

   • If you changed one component, did you notice any changes to any other components?

   • What component did you add that changed your game the most?

   • What component did you add that changed your game the least?

YOUTHS' SAMPLE PROJECTS: TOP-DOWN GAMES

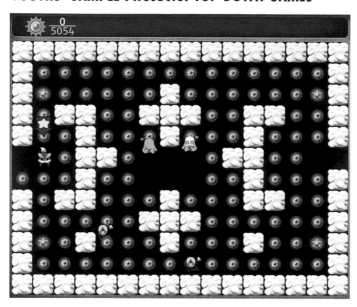

G*M game that models the space of Pac-Man

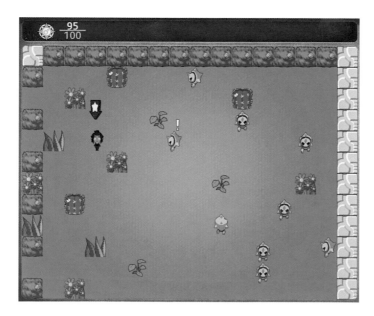

G*M game that models the space of Plants vs. Zombies

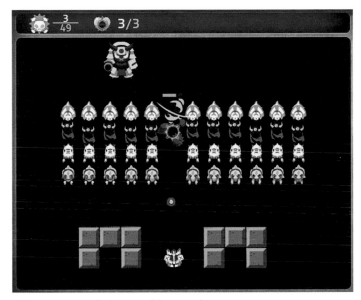

G*M game that models the space of Space Invaders

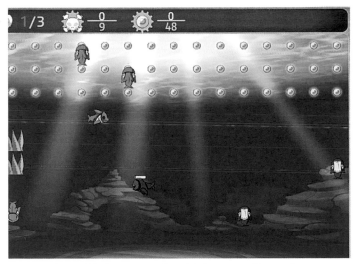

G*M game that models the ocean. (Credit: Ralph the Lazy Seal by UCFTyler)

WHAT TO EXPECT

At this point, youths should start to embrace thinking about game play in terms of a system rather than a causal chain of events. They also should be very familiar with the key terms and vocabulary of systems thinking and apply them to games.

Novice	Expert
• Thinks causally (rather than systematically) about components in the game (e.g., if you want the game to be harder, add a time limit) • Believes that changing the overall game play requires large changes in the behavior of the game components • Can identify components of the system but isn't clear about how changing one component affects the behavior of multiple other components; struggles to predict how the behavior of a component will be affected by a change to another component	• Sees the overall game-play experience (the function of the system) as being based on interactions among components (e.g., changing one component changes the game only to the extent that it affects the behaviors of other components) • Recognizes that sometimes a small change to a component can make a significant impact on the overall behavior of the system (game-play experience) • Has a sense of how components of the system interact and affect one another, and can predict these changes

Note Although youths do not need to finish *Episode 2* or *Episode 3* of the G*M Quests to participate in the modules, we highly recommend that they do so. Playing and fixing games increases their familiarity with the design tools and also gives them additional experiences of interaction. However, there is no G*M play time built into the rest of the curriculum, so if possible, youths should be encouraged to continue to work at home or in other spaces outside the group meetings.

VOICES FROM THE FIELD

It was especially refreshing to see the girls of the group taking on the task of designing a game and then iterating their design. In a field that is dominated by males, it was great to see these girls having a great time with Gamestar and thinking about the core components of game design.

—DEIDRA FLOYD, CENTRAL TEXAS WRITING PROJECT

DESIGN CHALLENGE 2, PART 2

TOP-DOWN VIDEO GAME EXAMPLES

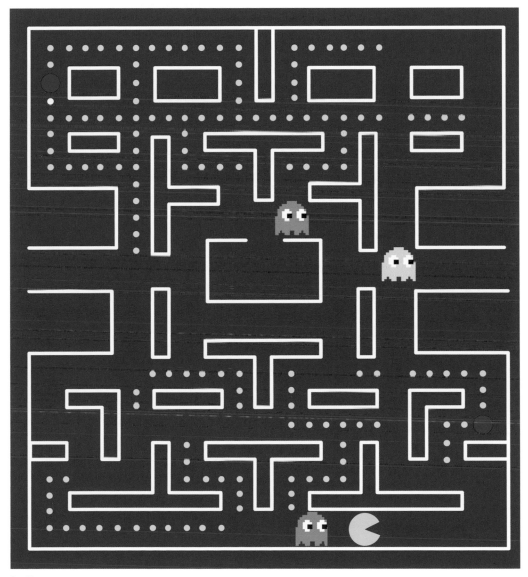

Pac-Man

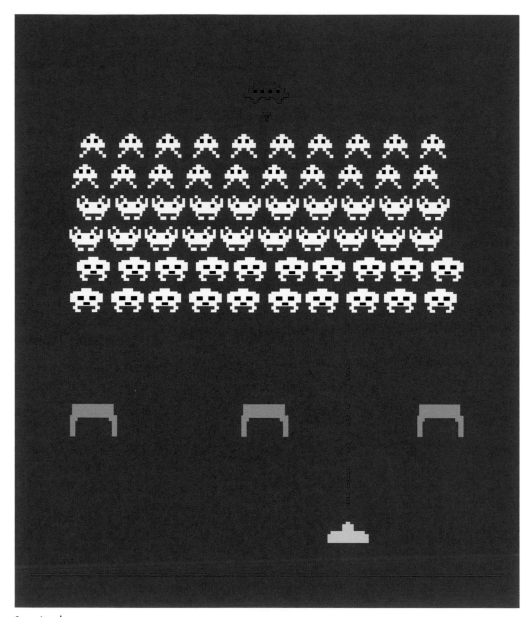

Space Invaders

Plants vs. Zombies

Total time: 185 minutes

OVERVIEW

The goal of this challenge is for youths to continue to develop their facility with game design tools and to consider games in terms of their properties as systems. In this challenge, they will add to their current conceptualization of systems by considering how the structure of a system is related to its function. By changing specific components and examining the impact on the overall system functioning, youths will continue to investigate the ways that interconnections among components work to build a system.

PRODUCT

Youths will design "platform" games in Gamestar Mechanic (G*M).

TARGETED SYSTEMS THINKING CONCEPTS

In this challenge, youths will continue to think about what makes a system work by analyzing the function of the game system. To do this, they will identify components of that game, identify the behaviors of those components, and finally, analyze how the behaviors of those components interconnect to create a specific way that the game functions. In addition, in this challenge, youths will start to consider how changes in a system's structure change the overall functioning of that system.

PARTS

PART 1: PLATFORM GAMES

In this part, youths will be introduced within G*M to a style of game known as a *platform* or *side-scroller*. The goal of this part is twofold: first, to introduce youths to a new kind of game that can broaden their design possibilities, and second, to continue developing their systems thinking vocabularies. The goal is for youths to start to see game design as a modeling activity, which involves creating a world that another person can explore through playing their game. Throughout the activity, youths should be encouraged to describe their designs in terms of the components that they have chosen, the behaviors of the components that they specified, how those behaviors interconnected, and especially how those interconnections affected the overall way their game functions.

Time: 30 minutes

PART 2: DESIGNING PLATFORM GAMES

The goal of this part is for youths to engage in designing a platform game and to start thinking about how changes that they make to components of the system change the overall way that the game functions.

Time: 110 minutes

PART 3: GOING BEYOND GAMES

In this final part of the challenge, youths will continue to think about how the structure of a system affects the way that it functions overall. In this case, they will think about system structure in the context of modeling (and fixing) a different system, called the Broken Lunchroom.

Time: 45 minutes

KEY DEFINITIONS

Identifying a system. A *system* is a collection of two or more components and processes that interconnect to function as a whole. Speed and comfort in a car for example are created by the interactions of the car's parts and thus are "greater than the sum" of all separate parts of the car. The way a system works is not the result of a single part but is produced by the interaction among the components and/or individual agents within it. A key way to differentiate things that are systems from things that aren't is to consider whether the overall way something works in the world will change if you remove one part of it.

Identify the way a system is functioning. The *function* of a system describes the overall behavior of the system—what it's doing or where it's going over time. A system's function might emerge naturally based on interconnections among components, or it might be the result of an intentional design (in which case we might also refer to the function of a system as its goal). Regardless, the function of a system is the result of the dynamics that occur among components' interconnected behaviors.

Distinguishing the goal of a system. The *goal* of the system is what it was intentionally designed to do. Sometimes this might be the same as the functioning of the system ... other times, the goal and the function are not aligned.

Identifying components. *Components* are the parts of a system that contribute to its functioning. Without being able to identify the parts of a system effectively, it's hard to understand how a system is actually working and how it might be changed.

Identifying behaviors. *Behaviors* are the specific actions or roles that a component of a system displays under various conditions. Being able to identify behaviors becomes important when we change systems because often a component will look the same after the change, but its behavior will be different.

Identifying interconnections. *Interconnections* are the different ways that a system's parts, or components, interact with each other through their behaviors and change the behaviors of other components through those interactions.

Considering the role of system structure. Understanding how a system's components are set up in relation to one another gives insight into the behavior of a component. A system's structure affects the behaviors of its components and the overall dynamics of a system. For instance, how a city's highway system is structured affects overall traffic patterns and car movement within it. Being able to see a system's structure gives insights into the mechanisms and relationships that are at the core of a system, which can be leveraged to create systemic changes.

Make systems visible. When we learn to "make the system visible"—whether modeling a system on the back of a napkin, through a computer simulation, a game, a picture, a diagram, a set of mathematical computations, or a story—we can use these representations to communicate about how things work. At their best, good pictures of systems help both the creator and the reader or audience to understand not only the parts of the system (the components), but also how those components work together to produce a whole.

COMMON CORE STATE STANDARDS COVERED — ENGLISH LANGUAGE ARTS

- RI.7.9
- W.6–8.3
- RST.6–8.3
- RST.6–8.7
- RST.6–8.9
- SL.6–12.4
- SL.7.5

NEXT GENERATION SCIENCE STANDARDS

- 3–5-ETS1–1
- 3–5-ETS1–2
- 3–5-ETS1–3
- MS-ETS1–1
- MS-ETS1–2
- MS-ETS1–4

MATERIALS OVERVIEW

- Digital projector
- Chart paper/whiteboard and markers
- Master sheet of G*M usernames and passwords.

HANDOUTS

- "Platform Video Game Examples"
- "Model of a System" (from Design Challenge 1)
- "What Makes a Good Game?" (from Design Challenge 1)
- "Playtester Feedback"
- "Broken Lunchroom"
- "Fix the Lunchroom"

OVERALL CHALLENGE PREPARATION

- Make sure to familiarize yourself with the Wrench tool in G*M
- Play and preload for projection one of the example platform games

PART 1: PLATFORM GAMES

In this part, youths will be introduced within G*M to a style of game known as a *platform* or *side-scroller*. The goal of this part is twofold: first, to introduce youths to a new kind of game that can broaden their design possibilities, and second, to continue developing their systems thinking vocabularies. The goal is for youths to start to see game design as a modeling activity, which involves creating a world that another person can explore through playing their game. Throughout the activity, youths should be encouraged to describe their designs in terms of the components that they have chosen, the behaviors of the components that they specified, how those behaviors interconnected, and especially how those interconnections affected the overall way their game functions.

Time: 30 minutes

STUFF TO HAVE HANDY

- Chart paper/whiteboard and markers

- One or more platform games, preloaded on a game system or on computers. When choosing a game, make sure that the game has real-world representations, such as trees or birds, or that models a real-world event, like a pandemic or war. **Note:** You might choose a single game that everyone will play or provide several different games for youths to explore. Possible choices might include:

  - Bud RedHead: The Time Chase (fantasy Platform, PC download): www .mediafire.com/download/9uflptq30ck8dds/budredhead -timechase.rar

  - The Fancy Pants Adventure World 2 (independent art/sketch Platform, Flash-based browser game): armorgames.com/play/553/the-fancy-pants -adventure-world-2

  - The Caverns of Hammerfest (simple vertical Platform, flash-based browser game): www.hfest.net/try.html#play

  In addition, the website www.platformgames.com provides a large selection of games for free online play.

HANDOUTS

HANDOUTS

- "Platform Video Game Examples"
- "Model of a System" (from Design Challenge 1)

RESEARCH: WHAT IS A PLATFORM GAME?—5 MINUTES

As a whole group, ask youths to reflect on the games that they created in Design Challenge 2 and to think about whether the games that they saw and built are representative of *all* the computer and video games that could be created (the answer is no!). Ask them to name some video games they know that are different. Then explain that today, they are going to learn to design a kind of game that isn't a bird's-eye view (top-down), but one that actually involves moving through space more as you do in real life, called a *platform* or *side-scroller game*. Ask if they have ever played games like that (if necessary, get them started by mentioning Super Mario Brothers, a side-scroller or platform game). Once you think that everyone has a vision of what a platform game might be, send them to their computers to experience these games for themselves.

PLAY: PLAY A PLATFORM GAME—10 MINUTES

At their computers, ask youths to spend about 10 minutes playing the platform game or games that you selected before the activity. Remember that youths with more experience playing video games will likely move through this task much more quickly than youths who have less experience. It is best that all youths complete at least one game, although experienced players can do more if they have time.

SHARE: FINDINGS ABOUT PLATFORM GAMES—15 MINUTES

After the youths play a platform game, engage them in a whole-group discussion. You may find it helpful to write down a list of the ideas that they brainstorm on chart paper or the board. The idea here is to provide youths with an opportunity to practice talking and thinking about games as systems, using the language introduced in Design Challenge 1. Use the "Model of a System" handout to guide the discussion.

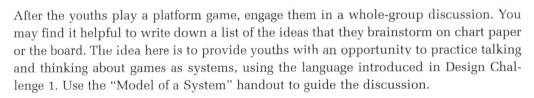

Points to discuss:

- Ask youths to help you identify components within the game that also can be found in the real world. For example, in a space with mountains, components might include different-sized hills, snow, grass, trees, mountain climbers, gold, and so on. In addition, you might focus the discussion on some of the new aspects that make platform games different from the top-down games that they created in Design Challenge 2. For example, platform games use *gravity* (you can jump and run), include *scrolling* (meaning that the game space extends beyond the visible screen), often involve collecting *items* or *points*, often have a complex win condition (e.g., players have to collect points *and* perform some action to reach the goal).

- Ask youths to think about the behaviors of those components and how those behaviors affect the function of the game that they just played.

- As a group, identify what might have motivated the game designers who created these games—what were the goals of the games that they designed? What were the designers trying to say about the world? What experience were they trying to foster in the players?

Note   It may be useful to point out that real-world objects (e.g., trees, birds, rocks) in the game that they just played can be represented in G*M using the existing sprites and backgrounds available. For example, combinations of stone and dirt blocks in G*M can be used to represent a mountain, or points can be used to represent gold.

DESIGN CHALLENGE 3, PART 1

PLATFORM VIDEO GAME EXAMPLES

Super Mario Brothers

Sonic the Hedgehog

PART 2: DESIGNING PLATFORM GAMES

The goal of part two is for youths to engage in designing a platform game and to develop an understanding about how changes they make to components of the system structure change the overall way that the game functions.

Time: 110 minutes

STUFF TO HAVE HANDY

- Digital projector
- Chart paper/whiteboard and markers
- Master sheet of G*M usernames and passwords

HANDOUTS

- "What Makes a Good Game?"
- "Playtester Feedback"

RESEARCH: PREPARING FOR DESIGN—10 MINUTES

Before youths begin to design, you'll want to give them a brief overview of how the tools work. This works best if you ask youths to turn off their monitors or close their laptops and project your computer for the whole group to follow the procedure together as you demonstrate it. The important difference between top-down and platform games can be explored using the level editor.

1. Introduce youths to the following elements:

   - Level settings

     - How to set the dimensions and orientation (vertical or horizontal) of a scrolling space

     - How to modify levels of gravity

     - How to select and change a background

   - Wrench tool

     - How to modify the properties of a sprite using the Wrench tool (i.e., by selecting the Wrench tool, then clicking a sprite)

   - Save button

     - This is very important, as youths can easily lose work if they forget to do this! The Save button is on the bottom right side of the editor.

2. After youths understand what the new tools are and how they work, prepare them to start thinking about the game that they are planning to design. You might want to remind them of the conversations that you have had in previous challenges about the various inspirations that game designers have for the games they create. If you wrote down a list of inspirations, you might want to show it again. If not, it's a good idea to do a little collective brainstorming before youths begin to design.

3. Encourage youths to make a plan for a platform game before they get involved with the tools. The plan can always change, but it's often helpful for youths to be at least somewhat intentional about their design, as the myriad tools and choices can easily become overwhelming. Some suggestions you might give them to help them get started might include the following:

   - Think about the game that they designed in Design Challenge 2, and what changes would be necessary to turn it into a platform game.

   - Use G*M to model the platform game that they just played.

   - Model another popular platform game that they have played in the past.

CREATE: DESIGN A GAME IN G*M—30 MINUTES

Once youths have a plan, they implement it by using the following process, which is designed to help them work mindfully:

1. Ask youths to get into pairs or small groups and discuss their game ideas. This can be done very quickly: many youths will still be unsure what their games will look like because they haven't had a chance to play with the new tools yet.

2. When they're ready, ask youths to log into G*M (**gamestarmechanic.com**). It would be useful to have your list of usernames and passwords handy (just in case!).

3. As in Design Challenge 2, for the next activity to work, youths *must* have redeemed a special code within G*M that provides access to the challenges in *Gaming the System*. Note that this only needs to be done once, so if they completed this step in Design Challenge 2, they can proceed directly to the next step. If this hasn't been done, direct them to follow this link: **gamestarmechanic.com/?activation =GAMINGTHESYSTEM**. They will be prompted to login (if they haven't already). They then click the Redeem button.

4.   Once youths are logged in, have them click on "WORKSHOP" and then "Challenges and Contests." Ask them to find the challenge called Platforming Perspective. This challenge shares the same format as the Top Down Perspective challenge (see image). Within the Platforming Perspective challenge area are four tabs that you will want to review briefly:

- "Challenge Missions" provides examples of top-down games for youths to play and explore (note that some have to be unlocked by completing easier games).

- "Design Brief" explains the rules and requirements for completing the challenge.

- "Create an Entry" is the design space where youths can go to create their own games.

- "Other Entries" is the storage area where their own and others' game entries are housed.

5. Give youths about 20 minutes to design their games in G*M. Encourage them to save their game frequently.

- You may want to remind them to think about how the sprites can be used to represent the different components of the space. Dirt blocks, for example, can be used to represent a mountain, points can be used to represent gold, etc.

- Youths might attempt to create multiple levels, so it may be helpful to constrain youths to create a game with only one level.

SHARE: PLAYTESTING — 25 MINUTES

After youths have designed their games, or at least have a version of a game that is playable, you will want to bring them together so they can prepare to give each other feedback. Depending on how often the youths in your group work together, you might need to add some atdditional scaffolding to help them ensure that they are giving productive, actionable feedback. See Design Challenge 1, pages 57–58 for more suggestions on encouraging positive feedback. Here, you may find it useful to model how to provide playtesting feedback first.

SUGGESTED APPROACH FOR MODELING PRODUCTIVE FEEDBACK

1. Go to Game Alley and open a platform game designed in G*M. Project the game so that youths can view and participate in the game play. **Note:** For this modeling activity, it is best *not* to play a game that one of your youths has designed. Instead, play a game that you have designed or a premade game found in Game Alley.

2. Ask youths to share "warm" and "cool" feedback about the game (see the section "Approach to Conversation and Critique in This Volume," pages 13–15, in the Introduction). For the "cool" feedback, be sure to emphasize that the feedback should include some suggestions for making changes as well. You might want to note that people feel encouraged to improve something that they have worked on when they feel *good* about it. A young designer especially can become discouraged without some positive comments and compliments about his or her design.

3. Pass out the "What Makes a Good Game?" worksheet from Design Challenge 1 and ask youths to think about the sample game from the framework of these categories, while continuing to emphasize the importance of offering both warm and cool feedback.

4. Explain to youths that they are about to play each other's games and encourage them to take playtesting very seriously. Stress that game designers learn from the feedback that their players give them—design is a constantly evolving process. Inform them that they are going to be using the same kind of structure that you just modeled.

PLAY AND SHARE: PLAYTESTING OTHERS' GAMES—20 MINUTES

Play: Separate youths into pairs and ask them to play each other's games for about 5 minutes. They will stay with this same partner for the following activities.

Share: Next, ask youths to take about two minutes to fill out the "Playtester Feedback" handout. **Note:** The "What Makes a Good Game?" handout can help guide their feedback as well. Encourage youths to provide detailed and constructive feedback:

- **Constructive:** "The core mechanics could be improved by decreasing the amount of repetition" helps the game designer understand what revisions to make.

- **Not Constructive:** "Your game's core mechanics are bad" is not helpful because it offers no specific suggestions for improvement.

At the conclusion of this independent writing activity, ask youths to take turns taking about 5 minutes each to share their feedback with their partners. It is important that the partners verbalize what they wrote. This gives the reviewer an opportunity to expand upon their feedback and gives each designer the opportunity to ask questions for clarification. Emphasize that *more* detail is better than *less* detail, and that all feedback should include both compliments about what's working in the design (warm feedback) and suggestions for improvement (cool feedback).

REFLECT AND ITERATE: REDESIGN IN G*M—15 MINUTES

Reflect: Finally, allow designers time to reflect about how they might revise their game in light of their peers' feedback. They can use the column on the right of the "Playtester Feedback" handout to make notes.

Encourage designers to think about *whether* and/or *how* to respond to each and every piece of feedback. Be sure that designers realize that they don't have to incorporate every piece of feedback into their revision. They are the final authority on their own games and have the right to disagree with any feedback that they receive.

Iterate: Provide time for youths to revise their games based on the "Playtester Feedback" results.

SHARE: LET'S TALK!—10 MINUTES

Now that youths have gone through one complete design cycle for their games, it's time to refocus on the game as a system. This discussion should help to focus youths not only on how games function as systems, but also on the importance of the structure of the system that they've designed and how changing a single component of the system can (although doesn't always) change the way the entire system functions. This conversation also can help them to think about the relationship between the function of the game and the actual goal that they set for their design.

Pass out the "Model of a System" worksheet from Design Challenge 1. Ask youths to take 5 minutes individually to map the game that they designed onto the model: What were the components, behaviors, interconnections, and overall function?

1. Have a few individuals explain their models to the whole group by displaying and playing them on the projector.

2. Use the following questions to facilitate discussion:

    •   What was the goal of the game?

    •   What are the components of the game?

    •   What behavior does each component display?

    •   How do the behaviors of the components interconnect and affect each other?

    •   How does the overall game function? Does it meet its goal?

3. Have youths think about their iteration process. Ask them to think about *one* thing that they changed from version 1 to version 2. How did that affect the overall game play (or the way that the game actually worked)? Ask this question of several youths, to extract the idea that a small change can lead to a significant outcome.

4. Tell youths that when they make a change to their game, they are actually changing the structure of the system—the way that the system's components are arranged in relation to one another. Ask them to think about how the structure of the system is related to the overall behavior or experience of the game, and how changing one aspect of the structure changes the overall experience of playing the game.

YOUTHS' SAMPLE PROJECTS: PLATFORM GAMES

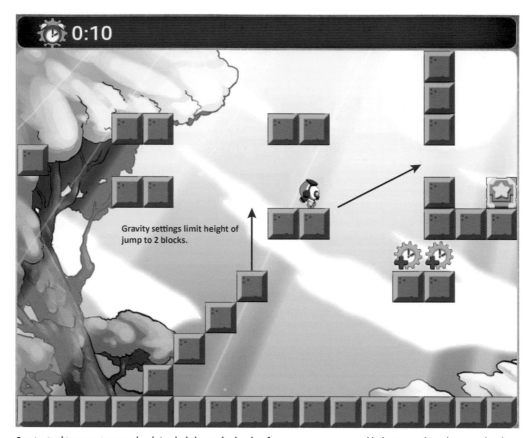

Gravity in this game is set to level 4, which limits the height of an avatar jump to two blocks. Notice how the game has been designed around this constraint, so that there is one clear path to the goal block, made up of two block intervals. The relationships between blocks are critical to success in this game. (Credit: *The Platform Challenge* by games)

Here, the avatar has fallen off the stair step and is now unable to reach the goal block, because of the relationship between gravity settings and the placement of the various platforms. (Credit: *The Platform Challenge* by games)

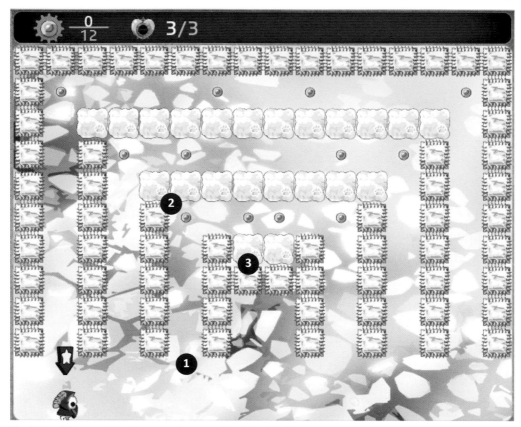

The design of this game is based on several very specific relationships between components:

1. The space to jump is just one block wide and bordered on both sides by dangerous damage blocks. This requires precision alignment by the avatar when preparing to jump.

2. Points are placed in a corner with damage blocks on two edges—a player must carefully guide the avatar while in mid-jump to avoid these obstacles.

3. There is a hidden goal block under the snow block, which will be revealed only upon contact.

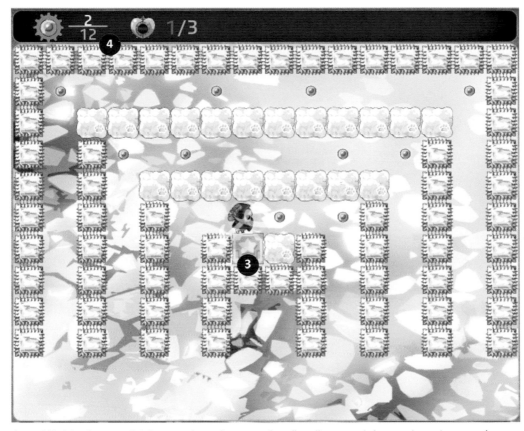

The goal block has been revealed, but notice that a player must also collect all 12 points before completing the game. There is a clear relationship between two separate win conditions, and both must be met.

3. Goal block

4. Point counter

(Credit: *You Have an Idea* by xlacombe592)

WHAT TO EXPECT

These ideas can be applied to both the whole-group discussion and the "Playtester Feedback" worksheet.

	Novice	Expert
Design-based thinking concepts	• Doesn't change one component at a time in an intentional way to see its effect • Doesn't know how to "test" a change to determine its impact • Thinks about each component of the game individually, rather than considering its interactions	• Changes one component of the game at a time to test its impact • Plays a game through to the end to determine the effect of particular design decisions • In designing, considers interactions among components and how they affect game play
Systems thinking concepts	• Thinks causally (rather than interactively) about components in the game; e.g., if you want it to be harder, add a time limit • Believes that changing the overall game play requires large changes in the behavior of the many components of the game • Doesn't understand how components of the system interact	• Sees the overall game play experience (the way that the system functions), as being based on interactions among components; e.g., changing one component changes the game only to the extent that it affects the behaviors of other components • Recognizes that sometimes a small change to a component can make a significant impact on the overall function of the system and the game-play experience • Has a sense of how components of the system interact and affect one another

DESIGN CHALLENGE 3, PART 2

PLAYTESTER FEEDBACK

Playtester's name: _____   Game name: _____

PLAYTESTER'S NOTES	DESIGNER'S REFLECTIONS
Share your general feedback with your partner. Be sure to include both what you liked and enjoyed about the game (warm feedback), and what you think could be changed to make it even better (cool feedback).	Notes:
Warm feedback:	
Cool feedback:	

Circle a number in each category to give the game designer feedback on his or her game.					Notes:

CHALLENGE   What was the level of challenge in the game?

1	2	3	4	5
Too easy				Too hard

AESTHETICS   Do the visual and audio designs support the game concept?

1	2	3	4	5
Does not support				Fully supports

DESIGN   How would you rate the design of the game space?

1	2	3	4	5
Weak				Fantastic

PACING   What do you think of the pacing of the game?

1	2	3	4	5
Too slow				Too fast

STORY   Does the story fit well with the game?

1	2	3	4	5
Not too well				Very well

PLAYTESTER'S NOTES	DESIGNER'S REFLECTIONS
What was challenging about the game?	Notes:
What suggestions do you have to make the game more difficult?	Notes:

PART 3: GOING BEYOND GAMES

In this final part of the challenge, youths will continue to think about how the structure of a system affects the way that it functions overall. In this case, they will look at system structure in the context of modeling (and fixing) a different system called the "Broken Lunchroom."

Time: 45 minutes

STUFF TO HAVE HANDY

- Digital projector

- Chart paper/whiteboard and markers

HANDOUTS

- "Broken Lunchroom"
- "Fix the Lunchroom"

RESEARCH: SETTING THE STAGE—15 MINUTES

The goal of this activity is to help youths start thinking about systems found in everyday life—taking the learning beyond game systems. Here, they are presented with a system that is broken, one where the designer's goal is not being met—in this case, an overcrowded and inefficient school lunchroom. The objective is for youths to conceptualize the problem as a system, examining the interconnections among components and how those interconnections are affecting the behavior of other components and the overall function of the system. Then youths can apply that analysis to hypothesizing solutions that would be most productive—and detailing why.

1. Gather all youths together and project the "Broken Lunchroom" worksheet. Explain that the goal of the next activity is to stretch the systems thinking skills that they have developed in their game designs and apply them to a new situation—and more important, to use their systems thinking skills to solve a real-world problem.

2. Read aloud the following scenario while youths examine the "Broken Lunchroom" worksheet:

> There is a problem in the cafeteria at Tunkin School: The lines move so slowly that sometimes students don't have time to eat their food before they have to go back to class. There are not enough lunch lines, and the existing lunch lines are uneven, with some lines being much longer than the others.
>
> This might be because students often get in the line that is closest to where they want to sit—most of them like to hang out with friends and eat on the side of the cafeteria that has more windows, which seems to make the situation even worse.
>
> In addition, the lunchroom is often congested from one class period to the next because students are not able to finish their lunch, throw away their trash, and return their trays before another lunch period begins. The administrators at Tunkin need to figure out how to solve this problem. What would you recommend?

3. Review the cafeteria diagram with the youths to make sure that they understand the symbols:

   • Each "X" in the diagram represents a person.

   • Areas of congestion are marked with yellow triangles.

   • Windows are represented by four-square grids.

   • The flow of events (get food, pay, eat, discard trash and trays, exit) is depicted by a number for each event.

4. Overall, make sure that youths can see the *narrative* of the story being represented in the images and employ the systems thinking language that the youths have been developing with the following points:

   • How is the system functioning? (It is congested.)

   • What are the components of the system? (People, tables, lunch line, windows, food counter, etc.)

   • What are the behaviors of those components? (The tables might block traffic, the lunch counter is the place that everyone needs to get to, etc.)

   • What do you think was the designed goal for the system? (To feed students, to provide a place to sit in groups, etc.)

5. Explain that in the next activity, youths are going to propose changes to the lunch-room system to improve how it functions, so that everyone has time to get lunch, eat, and clean up within their allotted lunch period.

   - There are some components of the system that cannot be changed. For example:

     - You can't remove the youths from the system.

     - Likewise, we don't have the funds to tear down the room and rebuild it, so doors and windows can't be added or taken away, and the food pickup counters must stay where they are, near the kitchens.

   - However, practically everything else could be changed and reconfigured to improve the function of the system.

6. Be sure that youths understand that their representations don't need to be works of art; they just need to *represent* their solutions as clearly as possible, so that another person could read and make sense of it.

7. Remind youths that in addition to drawing a "solution" to the problem, they need to explain in writing:

   - The changes they made to the lunchroom system at Tinkin School.

   - How the changes made will affect how the lunchroom system functions.

CREATE AND PLAY: FIXING THE BROKEN SYSTEM—20 MINUTES

Youths can work on the solutions either individually or in pairs. Pass out the "Fix the Lunchroom" handout, and either keep the "Broken Lunchroom" image projected or distribute copies. Before they begin, ask youths to brainstorm a hypothesis about what might be causing the problem. Their solutions should be based on that hypothesis.

Remind youths that they need to have a solution that is represented both as a picture and a written explanation. Monitor their progress, asking guided questions of individuals or pairs to ensure that their representation is clearly communicating what they think the new design should be.

SHARE: FINDING THE RIGHT FIX—10 MINUTES

Once youths complete the "Fix the Lunchroom" worksheet, conduct a whole-group debriefing of the solutions that emerged. This discussion can help youths to get feedback on their solutions and to give them practice in articulating their design ideas.

In the discussion, be sure to push on their thinking about interconnections—that is, *why* changing one component might affect another component, and thus the overall function of the system. You also can use this discussion to emphasize how, in changing the system structure, the overall functioning of the system is changing.

1. Either ask for volunteers or choose in advance a couple of solutions that seem somewhat different from each other.

2. Ask volunteers to come up to the front and project their solution (if possible), explaining what they changed in the lunchroom and why.

3. Encourage the use of systems thinking vocabulary, and specifically ask them to explain how particular components are interconnecting with other components. In so doing, ask youths to think about how the function of the system might change in relation to the change that they made to particular components.

4. You could use this opportunity to attune youths to the overall structure of the system (which components are included, how they are interconnecting, etc.), and how that structure leads to the broken and then-fixed function of the system (lunchroom).

WHAT TO EXPECT

These ideas can be applied to both the whole-group discussion and to the "Fix the Lunchroom" worksheet, if you choose to collect it.

	Novice	Expert
Systems thinking concepts	• Thinks causally (rather than interactively) about components in the system; e.g., if you take away tables, there will be more room • Believes that changing the overall system behavior requires making a big change (completely overhauling the entire configuration, rather than tweaking something small) • Doesn't articulate how components of the system interact	• Sees the overall system as being based on interactions among components; e.g., changing one component changes the system functioning only to the extent that it affects the behaviors of other components • Recognizes that sometimes a small change to a component can make a significant impact on the overall way that the system functions • Has a sense of how components of the system interact and affect one another

DESIGN CHALLENGE 3, PART 3

BROKEN LUNCHROOM

There is a problem in the cafeteria at Tunkin School: the lines move so slowly that sometimes students don't have time to eat their food before they have to go back to class. There are not enough lunch lines, and existing lunch lines are uneven, with some lines being much longer than the others.

This might be because students often get in the line that is closest to where they want to sit—most of their like to hang out with friends and eat on the side of the cafeteria that has more windows, which seems to make the situation even worse.

On top of this, the lunchroom is often congested from one class period to the next because students are not able to finish their lunch, throw away their trash, and return their trays before another lunch period begins. The administrators at Tunkin need to figure out how to resolve this problem. What would you recommend?

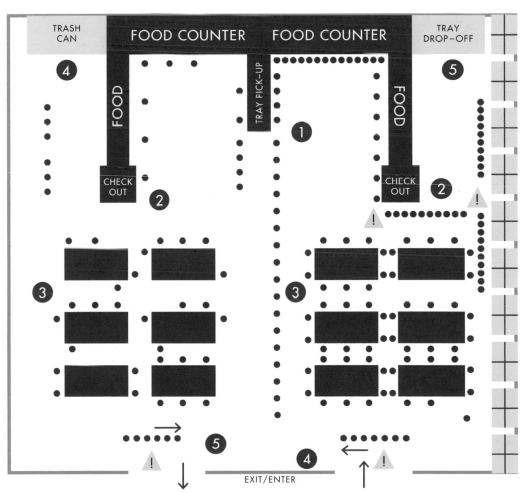

DESIGN CHALLENGE 3, PART 3

FIX THE LUNCHROOM

Using the diagram below, devise a solution to the problems in the Tunkin School lunchroom system:

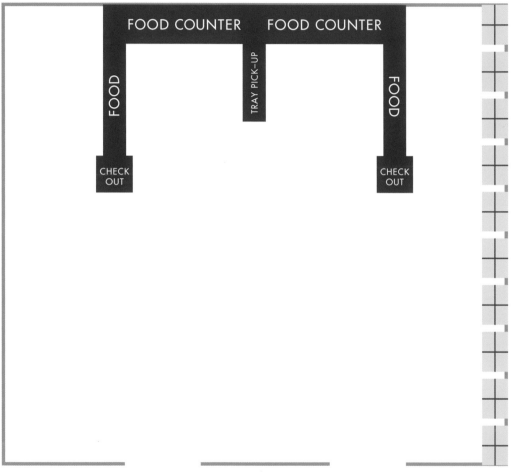

FOOD COUNTER   FOOD COUNTER

FOOD

TRAY PICK-UP

FOOD

CHECK OUT   CHECK OUT

EXIT/ENTER

What changes did you make to the lunchroom system?

How will the changes you made affect the lunchroom system?

DESIGN CHALLENGE 4
BALANCING THE GAME

Total time: 135 minutes

OVERVIEW

The goal of this challenge is for youths to better understand and practice using the key systems thinking idea of interconnections (that is, the concept that components within a system relate or are connected to other components in specific ways that determine how a system functions or the kinds of goals that it can meet). In game design, this is best expressed through the idea of balancing a game, which means making sure that a game's level of challenge is not too hard or too easy, and that the elements are all working well together to express the idea of the game. Ideally, youths should have completed at least half of *Episode 4: Gaining Perspective* in Gamestar Mechanic (G*M), by the start of this challenge.

PRODUCT

Youths will create games that have a design goal of being either extremely challenging or extremely easy.

TARGETED SYSTEMS THINKING CONCEPTS

In this challenge, youths will continue to think about how systems work by analyzing the goal of the system, as well as how the system is actually functioning, regardless of the goal of the game. They will identify components of that game, identify the behaviors of those components, and finally analyze how the behaviors of those components interconnect to create a specific way that the game functions, which may or may not meet the design goal that the creator had. Youths will start to think about how to change the overall function of the game (in this case, to make it more or less challenging) by considering the interconnections between components of the system.

PARTS

PART 1: CREATE THE EASIEST AND THE HARDEST GAME IN THE WORLD

In this part, youths will investigate the relationship between enemy sprite parameters and the level of challenge in a game, focusing on the theme of interconnections. Through modification of the speed, health, and damage parameters of avatar and enemy sprites, they will discover ways of balancing game play so that it is not too difficult or easy.

Time: 80 minutes

PART 2: PLAYTEST, REDESIGN, AND REFLECT

In this part, youths will playtest and refine their games. After that, they will reflect on how components of their system interconnected to balance their games, and consider the differences between difficult and easy games.

Time: 55 minutes

KEY DEFINITIONS

Identifying a system. Specifically, a *system* is a collection of two or more components and processes that interconnect to function as a whole. Speed and comfort in a car for example are created by the interactions of the car's parts and thus are "greater than the sum" of all separate parts of the car. The way a system works is not the result of a single part but is produced by the interaction among the components and/or individual agents within it. A key way to differentiate things that are systems from things that aren't is to consider whether the overall way something works in the world will change if you remove one part of it.

Identify the way a system is functioning. The *function* of a system describes the overall behavior of the system—what it's doing or where it's going over time. A system's function might emerge naturally based on interconnections among components, or it might be the result of an intentional design (in which case we also might refer to the function of a system as its *goal*). Regardless, the function of a system is the result of the dynamics that occur among system components' interconnected behaviors.

Distinguishing the goal of a system. The *goal* of the system is what a system that was intentionally designed is intended to do. Sometimes this might be the same as the functioning of the system ... other times the goal and the function are not aligned.

Identifying components. *Components* are the parts of a system that contribute to its functioning. Without being able to effectively identify the parts of a system, it's hard to understand how a system is actually working and how it might be changed.

Identifying behaviors. *Behaviors* are the specific actions or roles that a component of a system displays under various conditions. Being able to identify behaviors becomes important when we change systems because often a component will look the same after the change, but its behavior will be different.

Identifying interconnections. *Interconnections* are the different ways that a system's parts, or components, interact with each other through their behaviors, and through those interactions, change the behaviors of other components.

COMMON CORE STATE STANDARDS COVERED—ENGLISH LANGUAGE ARTS	NEXT GENERATION SCIENCE STANDARDS
• RI.7.9	• 3–5-ETS1–1
• W.6–8.3	• 3–5-ETS1–2
• RST.6–8.3	• 3–5-ETS1–3
• RST.6–8.7	• MS-ETS1–1
• RST.6–8.9	• MS-ETS1–2
• SL.6–12.4	• MS-ETS1–3
• SL.7.5	• MS-ETS1–4

MATERIALS OVERVIEW

STUFF TO HAVE HANDY

- Pencils or pens
- Digital projector
- Whiteboard/large piece of paper to write on
- Sample game in G*M open and ready to be edited

HANDOUTS

- "Speed and Balance"
- "Sample Parameter Combos"
- "Designer Notes"
- "Model of a System" from Design Challenge 1
- "Playtester Feedback"

PART 1: CREATE THE EASIEST AND THE HARDEST GAME IN THE WORLD

Youths will investigate the relationship between enemy sprite parameters and the level of challenge in a game, focusing on the theme of interconnections. Through modification of the speed, health, and damage parameters of avatar and enemy sprites they will discover ways of balancing game play so that it is not too difficult or easy.

Time: 80 minutes

STUFF TO HAVE HANDY

- Digital projector
- Sample game in G*M open and ready to be edited

HANDOUTS

- "Speed and Balance"
- "Sample Parameter Combos"
- "Designer Notes"
- "Model of a System" from Design Challenge 1

RESEARCH: SETTING THE STAGE—15 MINUTES

The objective of this first discussion is to prompt youths to think about the components of the games that they have been designing, specifically in terms of their interconnections. Game designers tune or balance their game so that it is not too easy or too hard for players to play, and work to create just the right amount of challenge. All games are made up of challenges or obstacles that a player must overcome to win the game. In this activity, we want youths to think about how this design goal of balance is achieved through interactions among the components of a game.

By this point, youths should have engaged in enough design practice to have a fairly clear memory or idea about the parameters available for most sprites. However, it would be useful for this discussion to have your G*M account open and projected on the wall or board, open to your Workshop area with a sample game up and ready for editing.

1. As a whole group, discuss the relationships between the following sprite behaviors:

   - Avatar speed and strength

   - Avatar health and enemy damage

   - Avatar speed and enemy speed

2. If your youths are familiar with video games, pass out (or display) and discuss the "Speed and Balance" and "Sample Parameter Combos" worksheets, which give examples of how to think about the speed and strength of video game characters in some well-known games and within G*M. **Note:** If the youths in your class aren't familiar with any of the characters on the "Speed and Balance" worksheet, feel free to substitute characters that they know better. The point is to help them to think about the ways that the characters' skills and abilities might look in G*M. Review these sheets as a class and make sure that everyone has a sense of the ways that particular attributes come together to make characters more or less formidable.

3. Ask youths to give an example of a relationship between avatar health and enemy damage that is unbalanced, meaning that a sprite (whether avatar or enemy) would have an unfair advantage or disadvantage. Ask youths what component or modification could be added to the unbalanced relationship to bring it back into balance (e.g., add health packs to the game to allow the avatar to heal itself, increase the health/strength of the avatar, decrease the amount of damage that an enemy can do, or change the game space so that an avatar can avoid an enemy more easily). Emphasize that there are many ways to establish balance, which is an emergent property that arises from the interconnections among game components, rather than being something that can be found in any given component of the game.

4. Check for youths' understanding. If any are struggling to grasp the concepts, you can build a game together in G*M and change the parameters to see the effects.

WHAT TO EXPECT

Although youths should have enough experience in G*M by now to understand the key characteristics of the sprites, not all of them might have thought about the ways that those characteristics interact. Youths who are avid game players might catch on to this interconnections concept more quickly than non-gamers, so you can incorporate that expertise into the conversation. What you want to look for in youths' responses is an awareness that changing one thing (e.g., enemy damage) interacts directly with some things (e.g., avatar health), but less directly with other things (e.g., avatar speed). In examining the interconnections among elements, youths start to notice that a simple change actually can cause a significant effect.

Novice	Expert
• Understands that components (such as the avatar or the enemy) have distinct behaviors that aren't tied to the larger game context • Understands how some behaviors directly interact with one another • Struggles with the notion of "balance" in a system • Doesn't think about interactions among more than two elements	• Has a sense of how components of the system interact and affect one another, and in particular, thinks about more than two elements interacting • Can describe what it means for a system to be "out of balance" • Understands how to bring systems back into balance • Recognizes that sometimes a small change to a component can make a significant impact on the overall way the system functions, in terms of game play

CREATE: DESIGNING THE EASIEST AND HARDEST GAMES IN THE WORLD!!! — 45 MINUTES

Building on your previous discussions of balance, ask youths to think about how they would design both the hardest and the easiest games in the world. Remind them that the hardest game in the world still has to be winnable! Pass out the "Designer Notes" handout so that youths can record how their two games differed when they made them extremely easy or extremely difficult.

Note that creating a challenging game easily could take youths many hours, so it will be useful to set some time constraints on this activity. It might make sense to ask everyone first to design the easiest game in the world, and then, after about 10 minutes, ask them to design the hardest game in the world.

It will be easier for youths to compare their easiest game with their hardest game if there are some overlapping parameters. For example, you might specify that both games meet all the following criteria:

• Must be top-down

• Must be able to be won in less than 3 minutes

• Must include (or cannot include) particular elements

When youths are ready to design, ask them to perform the following steps:

1. Log in to G*M (**gamestarmechanic.com**).

   As in the previous Design Challenges, for the next activity to work, youths *must* have redeemed a special code within G*M that provides access to the challenges in *Gaming the System*. If this hasn't been done, direct them to follow this link: **gamestarmechanic.com/?activation=GAMINGTHESYSTEM**. They will be prompted to login (if they haven't already). They then click the Redeem button.

2. Click on "Workshop" and then scroll down to "Challenges and Contests." Find the "Easy-Hard-Balanced" challenge. This challenge is designed exactly the same as the previous two; when youths are ready to design, they should click on the "Create an Entry" tab. Note that for each challenge youths can design only *one* game. However, they can include many levels in their games. You will want to ask youths to make different levels to represent their easy, hard, and balanced games.

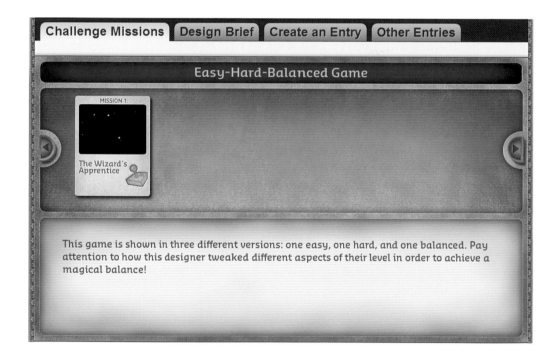

SHARE: WHAT MAKES A GAME EASY (OR HARD)?—20 MINUTES

After youths have completed their designs, bring everyone back together to talk about some commonalities across their games. Again, the goal here is for youths to focus on interconnections among components and how those interconnections work to shape the game-play experience (i.e., the function of the game). Difficult games don't just have more enemies; rather, the enemies might have particular traits that interconnect with other components of the game (such as the health of the avatar, the ways that the enemies move in the space, the time limit that players have to complete the goal, and other parts of the game that need to be completed). For the sharing of games made by youths:

1. Either ask for volunteers or select a couple of youths whose games share something in common. Ask them to come up to the front of the group and briefly share their games. When they have finished playing, ask the group to reflect on how each of the games worked, and what made the game easy. You might want to ask youths to take out the "Model of a System" handout from Design Challenge 1 (or pass it out to any youth who doesn't have it).

2. Ask the group to analyze the game in terms of its design goal, its components, their behaviors, and the ways that those behaviors interconnect. This is likely to be a quick conversation, as there are many fewer interconnections for easy games as for challenging ones.

3. Repeat this same presentation-analysis cycle for challenging games. Note that challenging games will have many more interconnections to discuss, so you might ask fewer youths to share their "hard" games.

VOICES FROM THE FIELD

It was interesting for me to have the youths share their thoughts on why a game is easy. I attempted to use it as an opportunity to illustrate that an easy game has a simple goal with very few components and very simple interactions versus a difficult game that has many components with many complex relationships that have multiple pathways to achieving the goal created by the designer.

—TRAVIS POWELL, OREGON WRITING PROJECT

DESIGN CHALLENGE 4, PART 1

SPEED AND STRENGTH

	Character	Speed	Health
Scribblenauts	Maxwell	0 1 2 3 4 5 6 7 8 9 10	1 2 3 4 5
Zelda	Link	0 1 2 3 4 5 6 7 8 9 10	1 2 3 4 5
Cooking Mama	Cooking Mama	0 1 2 3 4 5 6 7 8 9 10	1 2 3 4 5
Little Big Planet	Sackboy	0 1 2 3 4 5 6 7 8 9 10	1 2 3 4 5
Sonic the Hedgehog	Sonic	0 1 2 3 4 5 6 7 8 9 10	1 2 3 4 5

More information on these characters can be found at the following links:

- Scribblenauts: games.kidswb.com/official-site/scribblenauts/unlimited/home.html?lang=en
- Link: zelda.com/universe/pedia/l.jsp
- Cooking Mama: cookingmama.com

SAMPLE PROJECTS: BALANCE

The game label shows us how carefully the designer of this game has thought through, and balanced, the various win conditions of his or her game. To win this game, you must be nearly perfect as a player—despite its apparent simplicity, it is perfectly balanced in terms of the challenge! (Credit: *Cowboys in the Snow* by Blankenshipl)

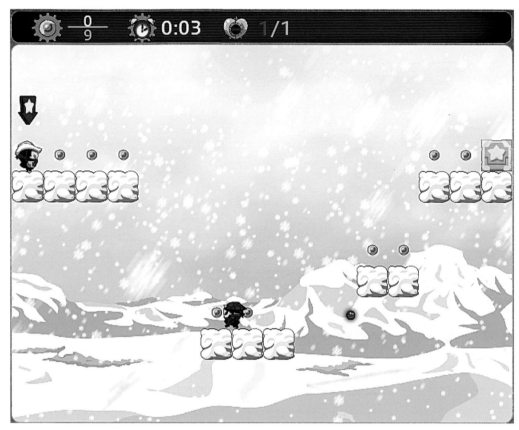

How hard can a game with a single enemy be? While the number of components in this game is small, their placement and attributes have been thought through carefully. The speed of the enemy is set to 4 (very fast!), which gives a player only a fraction of a second to land on the platform and rebound to the next. The distance between platforms is perfectly matched to the gravity settings, meaning the avatar can jump just high enough (and no higher) to reach the upper platforms. Every component has been balanced in relation to every other component to create a game with a perfect level of challenge. (Credit: Cowboys in the Snow by Blankenship!)

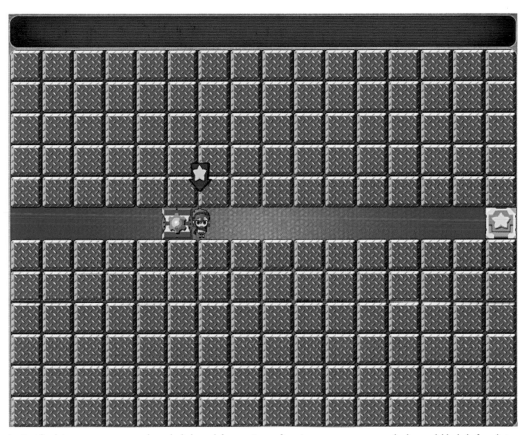

In Squish, three components are elegantly balanced for maximum fun: An avatar races to reach the goal block before being overtaken by the moving block to its left. Here, the speed of the moving block and avatar had to be balanced carefully to ensure that the avatar could outrun the advancing block (but just barely). (Credit: Squish by Destro15)

SAMPLE PROJECTS: EASIEST AND HARDEST GAMES

The game label gives some clues as to what makes this puzzle game challenging. (Credit: Key to Victory by Maxwellstone)

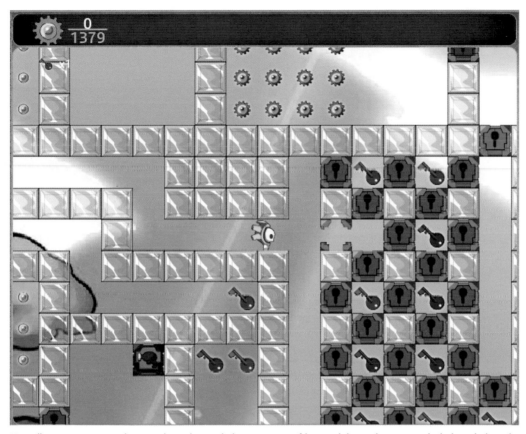

Maxwellstone creates a complex maze by working with the components of keys and doors; players must think through the order in which keys are collected and doors unlocked, or they will remain trapped in the maze forever (or until you stop playing, anyway). (Credit: Key to Victory by Maxwellstone)

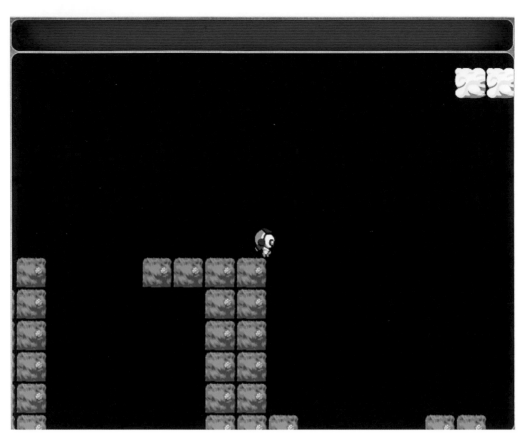

Easy4 is a platform game that uses a minimum number of components to maximum effect. A player has one action to take in the game—jumping—but he or she must do so carefully. The bottom edge of the game space is unbounded, and failing to land on a platform means sudden death. (Credit: Easy4 by nmak1999)

DESIGN CHALLENGE 4, PART 1

SAMPLE PARAMETER COMBOS

Parameter Combo 1: Juror Nemesis

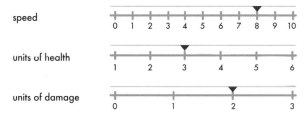

Juror Nemesis moves super fast, has medium health, and is quite powerful

Parameter Combo 2: Juror Nemesis

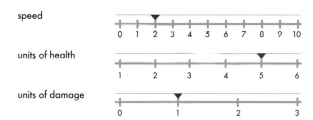

Juror Nemesis moves slowly, is hearty but not very strong

Parameter Combo 3: Juror Nemesis

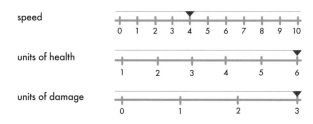

Juror Nemesis moves at an average speed, is super healthy and very powerful

DESIGN CHALLENGE 4, PART 1

DESIGNER NOTES

THE EASIEST GAME IN THE WORLD!

List the components that you included to create your easiest game.

What made this game so easy?

THE HARDEST GAME IN THE WORLD!

List the components that you included to create your hardest game.

How is your hardest game different from your easiest game?

What made this game so challenging?

PART 2: PLAYTEST, REDESIGN, AND REFLECT

In this part, youths will playtest and refine their games. After this, they will revisit the earlier conversation about systems to reflect on how components of their system interconnected to balance their games, and consider the differences between difficult and easy games.

Time: 55 minutes

STUFF TO HAVE HANDY

*   Digital projector

HANDOUTS

*   "Playtester Feedback"

RESEARCH: PREPARING FOR PLAYTESTING—10 MINUTES

After youths have designed their games (or at least have a version of a game that is playable), you will want to bring them together so they can prepare to give each other feedback on their games. This playtesting episode will mirror the playtesting from Design Challenge 3 and uses the same "Playtester Feedback" form that was used in that challenge. It is useful to review that handout and help the youths think about the kinds of feedback that will be helpful for designers who are thinking specifically about balancing the level of challenge.

SUGGESTIONS FOR MODELING CONSTRUCTIVE FEEDBACK:

1. Go to Game Alley and open a platform-style game designed in G*M. Project your computer screen so that youths can participate in the game play (for this, it is best *not* to play a game that one of your youths has designed).

2. Ask youths to share "warm" and "cool" feedback about the game (see the section "Approach to Conversation and Critique in This Volume" in the Introduction, pages 13–15). Be sure to emphasize that the "cool" feedback should include some suggestions for making changes as well. You might want to note that people feel

encouraged to improve something that they have worked on when they feel good about it; if they don't have some positive feelings and compliments about their design, it is easy to get discouraged.

3. Ask youths to think about which components are interconnecting to make the game challenging. Then encourage them to think about how they might change the game to make it more (or less) challenging. If they are having trouble, you can offer some more specific prompts, including the following:

    •   How much health did the avatar have? How strong were the enemies? Did this seem like a good balance between health and damage?

    •   Were there any enemies that seemed unbalanced, either too fast or too strong, or defeated the avatar too easily?

    •   Were there ways for you to "power up" your avatar, to make it stronger or faster or more able to defeat the enemies? Did you think that it was important to have these kinds of power-ups in the game? If so, why?

4. Explain to youths that they are about to play each other's games. Encourage them to take playtesting very seriously, and inform them that they are going to be using the same kind of structure that you just modeled as a whole group.

PLAY, SHARE, AND REFLECT: PLAYTESTING OTHERS' GAMES — 20 MINUTES

Professional game designers learn constantly from the feedback on their games that they get from their players. In this activity, youths will get a twofold benefit from this practice as they explore each other's designs and learn what their peers think about their own.

1. Pair up youths and ask them to play each other's games for about 5 minutes.

2. When the 5 minutes are up, ask partners to fill out the "Playtester Feedback" handout. Encourage them to provide detailed, constructive feedback, using the handout to organize their thinking.

3. After about 5 minutes of independent writing, ask youths to take turns sharing their feedback. Be sure that they are *not* just passing their forms to each other, but that each reviewer actually reads the feedback aloud so that the designer is able to listen to it and ask questions for clarification. Be sure to emphasize that *more* detail is better than *less* detail, and that all feedback should include both compliments (warm feedback) and suggestions for improvement (cool feedback).

WHAT TO EXPECT

The open-ended questions at the bottom of the worksheet provide a place where you can begin to see how youths are thinking about the overall function of the game and whether it is meeting its design goal. How challenging a game is provides a good indication of the "state" of the system; that is, how the game functions overall. Youths who are still struggling to understand interconnections might think specifically about what makes a game challenging ("There were so many enemies!" or "The time was so short!").

Novice	Expert
• Thinks about challenge as being caused by a single component	• Thinks about challenge as being an interaction among the behaviors of components • Can specify how changing one behavior might affect another component, and therefore the overall function (i.e., the challenge level) of the game

Note More expert systems thinkers recognize that particular characteristics are challenging only insofar as they interact with other elements. For example, a time is only too short relative to what needs to be accomplished in that time.

ITERATE: REDESIGN IN G*M—15 MINUTES

Ask youths to revise their games based on the results of the playtester feedback.

SHARE: WHAT MAKES A GAME EASY (OR HARD)?—10 MINUTES

After youths have completed their designs, bring everyone back together to talk about some commonalities across their games. This can be a more abbreviated version of the conversation from Part 1; the goal here is to focus on the impact that any changes that youths made to components in their games might have had on the overall level of challenge in the game.

1. Either ask for volunteers or choose one or two youths who made significant changes to their games. Invite them to play their games while the entire group observes.

2. Ask the designers to explain what changes they made and what effect those changes had (i.e., whether they made the game easier or more difficult).

3. Ask the group if they can explain why those changes served to make the game easier or harder. Specifically, prompt the group to start to talk about the interconnections that emerge between two or more components. Some example questions might include:

   • Why would adding a time limit make the game more difficult? How does time affect other parts of the game?

   • Why would adding more blocks around the goal make the game more difficult? What else is affected by putting more blocks there?

   • Why does reducing the health of the avatar make the game more difficult? What happens to the avatar in relation to its enemies when you do that?

DESIGN CHALLENGE 4, PART 2

PLAYTESTER FEEDBACK

Playtester's name: _____   Game name: _____

PLAYTESTER'S NOTES	DESIGNER'S REFLECTION
Be sure to include both what you liked and enjoyed about the game (warm feedback), and what you think could be changed to make it even better (cool feedback). Warm feedback: Cool feedback:	Notes:
Below, circle a number in each category to give the game designer feedback on his or her game. **CHALLENGE** What was the level of challenge in the game? 1 2 3 4 5 Too easy Too hard **AESTHETICS** Does the visual and audio design support the game concept? 1 2 3 4 5 Does not support Fully supports **DESIGN** How would you rate the design of the game space? 1 2 3 4 5 Weak Fantastic **PACING** What do you think of the pacing of the game? 1 2 3 4 5 Too slow Too fast **STORY** Does the story fit well with the game? 1 2 3 4 5 Not too well Very well	Notes:

PLAYTESTER'S NOTES	DESIGNER'S REFLECTIONS
What was challenging about the game?	Notes:
What suggestions do you have to make the game more difficult?	Notes:

Total time: 130 minutes

OVERVIEW

This challenge creates an opportunity for youths to experiment directly with the interconnections that arise between two specific components: enemy sprites and block sprites. Youths will practice creating different kinds of movement and mechanics by adjusting enemy sprite parameters (i.e., movement style, start direction, and turn direction). They will be encouraged to consider how the qualities of the game space influence and determine the kinds of movement that is possible.

PRODUCT

Youths will design games that focus specifically on the interconnections between enemy movement and the creation of the game space.

TARGETED SYSTEMS THINKING CONCEPTS

In this challenge, youths will continue to think about what makes a system function by experimenting with interconnections between particular components.

PARTS

PART 1: UNDERSTANDING MOVEMENT PATTERNS

In this part, youths will explore interconnections by creating games with a design goal of including complex patterns of enemy movement, with the purpose of exploring the concept that movement is a system defined by a number of component variables: speed, start direction, turn direction, patrolling, and block placement.

Time: 80 minutes

PART 2: PLAYTEST, REDESIGN, AND REFLECT

In this part, youths will playtest and refine their games and then reflect on how the components of their systems are interconnected. This exploration also will revisit how enemy movement is related to how difficult or easy their games could be.

Time: 50 minutes

KEY DEFINITIONS

Identify the way a system is functioning. The *function* of a system describes the overall behavior of the system—what it is doing or where it's going over time. A system's function might emerge naturally based on interconnections among components, or it might be the result of an intentional design (in which case, we might also refer to the function of a system as its goal). Regardless, the function of a system is the result of the dynamics that occur among components' interconnected behaviors.

Identifying components. *Components* are the parts of a system that contribute to its functioning. Without being able to effectively identify the parts of a system, it's hard to understand how a system is actually working and how it might be changed.

Identifying behaviors. *Behaviors* are the specific actions or roles that a component of a system displays under various conditions. Being able to identify behaviors becomes important when we change systems, as often a component will look the same after the change but its behavior will be different.

Identifying interconnections. Interconnections are the different ways that a system's parts, or components, interact with each other through their behaviors, and through those interactions, change the behaviors of other components.

COMMON CORE STATE STANDARDS COVERED—ENGLISH LANGUAGE ARTS	NEXT GENERATION SCIENCE STANDARDS
• RI.7.9	• 3–5-ETS1–1
• W.6–8.3	• 3–5-ETS1–2
• RST.6–8.3	• 3–5-ETS1–3
• RST.6–8.7	• MS-ETS1–1
• RST.6–8.9	• MS-ETS1–2
• SL.6–12.4	• MS-ETS1–3
• SL.7.5	• MS-ETS1–4

MATERIALS OVERVIEW

- Pencils, pens, or colored pencils
- Digital projector

HANDOUTS

- "Movement Patterns" worksheets (1–4)
- "Enemy Movement in Space Reflection"
- "Playtester Feedback"

OVERALL CHALLENGE PREPARATION

- Go to the Gamestar Mechanic (G*M) Workshop, choose an enemy, and set up a demo to model its movement patterns for your youths on a projector.

PART 1: UNDERSTANDING MOVEMENT PATTERNS

In this part, youths will explore interconnections by creating games with a design goal of including complex patterns of enemy movement, for the purpose of exploring the concept that movement is a system defined by a number of component variables: speed, start direction, turn direction, patrolling, and block placement.

Time: 80 minutes

STUFF TO HAVE HANDY:

- Digital projector
- Pencils, pens, or colored pencils

HANDOUTS

- "Movement Patterns" worksheets (1–4)
- "Enemy Movement in Space Reflection"

VOICES FROM THE FIELD

To illustrate the importance of patterns, I used a simple top-down example of an enemy that made a right turn when it bumped into things. The sprite made four 90-degree turns and then repeated the process. I took a block and placed it in the path of the sprite to change its pattern and movement in the game space.

—TRAVIS POWELL, OREGON WRITING PROJECT

RESEARCH: THINKING ABOUT ENEMY MOVEMENT—10 MINUTES

In this activity, prepare youths to think about the movements of their enemy sprites and how to create complex patterns from simple behaviors.

1. Project your demo of enemy movements to the group.

2. Ask youths to observe the movement of the enemy. For example, does it turn right or left every time it hits an obstacle? Does it turn at random? Does it patrol?

3. Ask youths to describe aloud to the group what they notice about the patterns of enemy movement. (You may want to show several different configurations of enemy movement.)

4. Encourage youths to think of enemy movement as having many different behaviors (e.g., speed, start direction, turn direction, patrolling, and block placement).

Note Youths often find the patrol settings to be a bit confusing. If you have time, you can help them to understand this concept better by creating and demonstrating four blocks of patrolling enemies on the screen, each with a different turn radius. By comparing the movement of each enemy, youths will better understand how patrolling works.)

5. Inform youths that today, they will be tasked to create games with complex patterns of enemy movement.

VOICES FROM THE FIELD

I emphasized that being able to recognize patterns and being able to identify multiple patterns and those relationships gives us predictability, and with that, we are able to develop a successful strategy to maneuver through the game space.

—TRAVIS POWELL, OREGON WRITING PROJECT

IMAGINE: CREATING A DESIGN PLAN FOR ENEMY MOVEMENT—10 MINUTES

In this set of activities, youths will use paper worksheets to plan movement patterns in their game.

1. Pass out the "Movement Patterns" worksheets 1–4 to all youths.

2. Choose one of the parameters that youths just studied (speed, start direction, turn direction, patrolling, or block placement) for an enemy, and then have them sketch out a movement pattern that they are sure can be created using the design tools in G*M. **Note:** You might need to help them think about how they represent an enemy and the enemy's movement. As a group, you might want to come up with symbols that indicate movements. For example, direction (with arrows), speed (arrows with more lines versus fewer lines, or with dotted lines), and patrolling (continuous loops indicating a pattern). It might be useful to review "Movement Patterns Worksheet 1" as a whole group before they begin.

3. Encourage youths who have demonstrated an advanced understanding of enemy movement patterns to work with multiple enemies, each with a different movement pattern.

4. Note that "Movement Patterns Worksheet 4" is a true design document, where youths can think about both how they want enemies to move and how the space, as they design it, affects that movement. This is the document that they will work with when designing their game in G*M.

Note   As youths are working on this activity, you will want to move around to make sure that everyone is thinking about the interconnections between enemy movements and block placement. If you think that some youths are still a bit unsure about the connection, it would be good to review some sample movement patterns worksheets as a group before proceeding to the next exercise.

CREATE: BUILD A GAME—30 MINUTES

Using the plans that youths had for enemy movements, they will test them out in the game.

1. Once youths have finished sketching out the movement pattern on the worksheet, have them log into G*M to create a game that brings the movement patterns to life (with the blocks and enemies).

2. As in the previous Design Challenges, for the next activity to work, youths *must* have redeemed a special code within G*M that provides access to the challenges in *Gaming the System*. Note that this only needs to be done once, so if they completed this step in an earlier Design Challenge, they can proceed directly to the next step. If this hasn't been done, direct them to follow this link: **gamestar mechanic.com/?activation=GAMINGTHESYSTEM**. They will be prompted to login (if they aren't already). They then click the Redeem button.

3. Once youths are logged in, have them click on "Workshop" and then on "Design Around An Enemy." Like the previous challenges, when youths are ready to design, they should click on the "Create an Entry" tab.

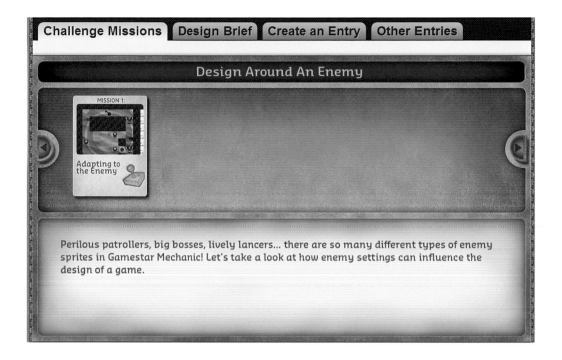

| Challenge Missions | Design Brief | Create an Entry | Other Entries |

Design Around An Enemy

MISSION 1:

Adapting to the Enemy

Perilous patrollers, big bosses, lively lancers... there are so many different types of enemy sprites in Gamestar Mechanic! Let's take a look at how enemy settings can influence the design of a game.

4. Encourage all youths to think about applying the same kind of movement pattern to multiple sprites to see what kinds of predictable (or unpredictable!) patterns that they can create.

5. Suggest that they explore several different kinds of movement patterns in the same game, and ask them to compare the patterns that they created in the game to their drawings.

REFLECT AND SHARE: INTERCONNECTIONS—30 MINUTES

As youths wrap up their games, they will reflect and share their understanding with others as an important part of the process.

1. Have youths reflect on what they've been doing by taking notes on the "Enemy Movement in Space Reflection" worksheet. Ask them to be very detailed, as these notes will help them when they are sharing their ideas with the entire group.

2. After about 10 minutes, gather your group together and ask for three volunteers to present their sketched (from "Movement Patterns" worksheet 4) and actual games. Encourage the youths to think about covering the following questions as they make their presentations:

   • Why did you choose a particular movement pattern? How did you decide: (a) which enemy to use, and (b) where in the game space to place that enemy?

   • Did anything surprising happen when you were creating patterns?

   • What was the most interesting pattern that was created?

   • What do you think you can say about the interconnections that you formed between the enemy (or enemies) in your game and the way that you placed the blocks?

WHAT TO EXPECT

These ideas can be applied to both the whole-group discussion/individual reflection, as well as to the "Playtester Feedback" handout, discussed later.

Novice	Expert
• Preoccupied with number of enemies and places little emphasis on their movement • Places emphasis on only one aspect of enemy movement (e.g., speed) • Incorporates enemies, but restricts movement and/or location of them to a small area of the game space. Focuses on enemy movement in terms of placement and direction of travel while paying little to no attention to interaction between enemies and elements of game space (e.g., structuring movement via block placement).	• Shows the understanding that enemies can present a challenge beyond the sheer number of them that are present (i.e., via tactical creation of movement patterns) • Attends to two or more elements of enemy movement (i.e., speed, start direction, turn direction, and patrolling) to establish movement pattern in the game that presents an effective challenge • Establishes enemy movement patterns that effectively create challenges across the game space (with respect to the design goal of the game) • Very attentive to any interactions between enemies and the elements of game space (e.g., structuring movement via block placement)

SAMPLE PROJECTS: PATTERNS AND MOVEMENT

PATROLLING

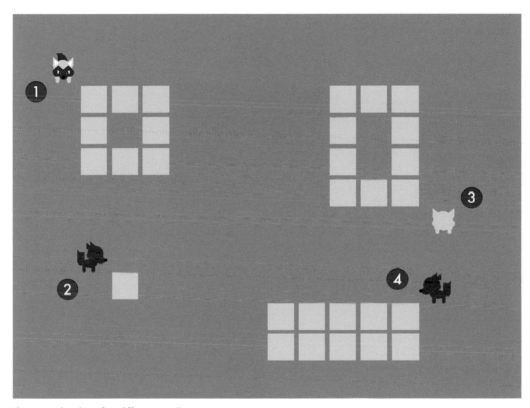

This screen shot shows four different patrolling movement patterns.

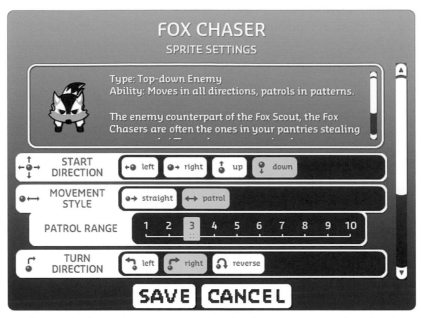

1. In this example, the Fox Chaser enemy moves *down* when the game starts, moves five cells and turns *left,* moves another five cells and turns *left,* and so on.

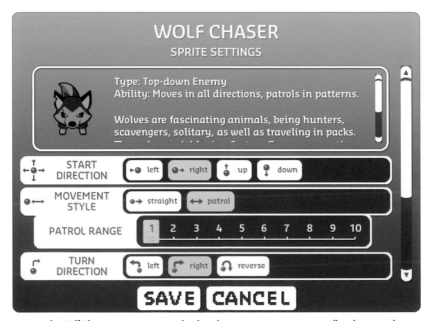

2. Here, the Wolf Chaser enemy moves *right* when the game starts, moves one cell and turns *right,* moves another cell and turns *right,* and so on.

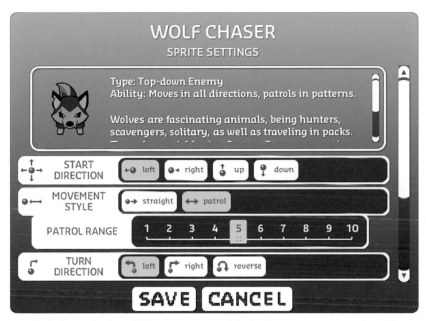

3. In the third example, the Wolf Chaser enemy moves *left* when the game starts, moves five cells and turns *left,* moves another five cells and turns *left,* and so on.

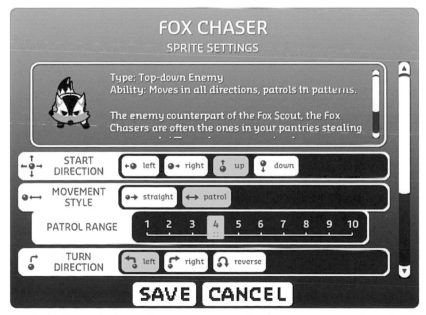

4. In the fourth example, the Fox Chaser enemy moves *up* when the game starts, moves four cells and turns *left,* moves another four cells and turns *left,* and so on.

PATTERN MOVEMENT

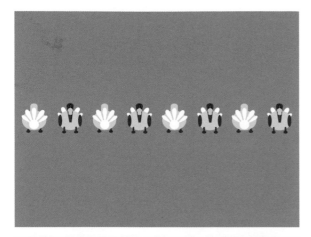

Enemies can reverse direction when they encounter an obstacle or edge. In this example, the movement of eight Fox Chaser enemies creates an interesting pattern because every enemy moves in the same direction (up-down-up-down-up-down-up-down).

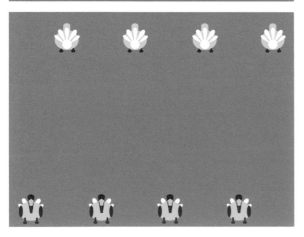

DESIGN CHALLENGE 5, PART 1

MOVEMENT PATTERNS WORKSHEET 1

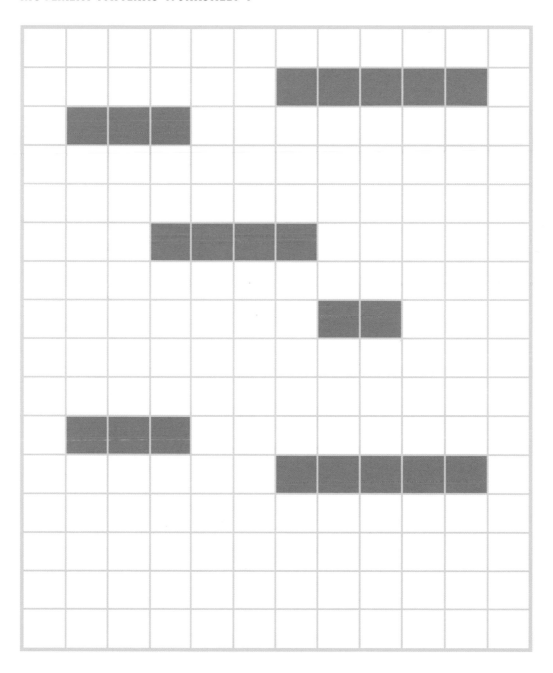

MOVEMENT PATTERNS WORKSHEET 2

MOVEMENT PATTERNS WORKSHEET 3

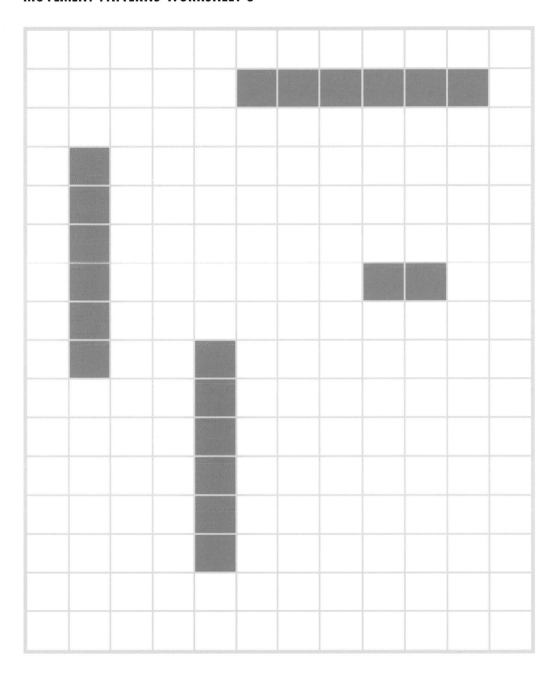

MOVEMENT PATTERNS WORKSHEET 4

ENEMY MOVEMENT IN SPACE REFLECTION

1. Why did you choose a particular movement pattern for your enemy (or enemies)?

2. How did the movement pattern relate to where in the game space you decided to place the enemy?

3. How did the movement pattern relate to how you designed the game space (for example, where you placed the blocks)?

4. When you translated your sketch from "Movement Patterns Worksheet 4" into G*M, did you have to make any changes? If so, why were they necessary?

PART 2: PLAYTEST, REDESIGN, AND REFLECT

In this part, youths will playtest and refine their games and then reflect on how components of their system are interconnected. This exploration also will revisit how enemy movement is related to how difficult or easy their games could be.

Time: 50 minutes

STUFF TO HAVE HANDY

- Digital projector

HANDOUTS

- "Playtester Feedback"

RESEARCH: PREPARING FOR PLAYTESTING—5 MINUTES

By now, youths should be very comfortable with playtesting and iterating, but as usual, it's a good idea to prepare everyone formally for this next exercise. In this case, youths

need to focus on how well the enemy movement interconnects with the placement of the blocks. You will want to introduce them to this specific design goal before they begin to playtest each other's games.

Remind youths of the importance of sharing both "warm" and "cool" feedback about the game (see the section "Approach to Conversation and Critique in This Volume" in the Introduction, pages 13–15). For the "cool" feedback, be sure to emphasize that the feedback should include some suggestions for making changes as well. You might want to note that people feel encouraged to improve something that they have worked on when they feel good about it; if they don't have some positive feelings and compliments about their design, it is easy to get discouraged.

PLAY, SHARE, AND REFLECT: PLAYTESTING OTHERS' GAMES—20 MINUTES

Take a few moments to allow youths to playtest one another's games to see how their peers are doing and utilize effective feedback practices.

1. Pair up youths and ask them to play each other's games for about 5 minutes.

2. When the 5 minutes are up, ask partners to fill out the "Playtester Feedback" handout. Encourage reviewers to provide detailed, constructive feedback.

3. After about 5 minutes of independent writing, ask the youths to take turns sharing their feedback. Be sure that they are *not* just passing their forms to each other, but that each reviewer reads the feedback aloud, with the designer able to ask questions for clarification. Be sure to emphasize that *more* detail is better than *less* detail, and that all feedback should include both compliments (warm feedback) and suggestions for improvement (cool feedback).

ITERATE: REDESIGN IN G*M — 15 MINUTES

Ask youths to revise their games based on the results of the playtester feedback.

SHARE: INTERCONNECTIONS — 10 MINUTES

The goal of this final whole-group discussion is to think about the interconnections that youths have observed and to help them start to think about the relationship between interconnections and overall system functioning as a whole.

1. Either ask for volunteers or choose one or two youths who made significant changes to their games. Invite them to play their games for the entire group.

2. Ask presenters to explain what changes they made and the effects those changes had on the interconnection between the enemy movement and the design or layout of the space. Encourage the youths to think about the following questions as they make their presentations:

   - Why did you choose a particular movement pattern? How did you decide: (a) which enemy to use, and (b) where in the game space to place that enemy?

   - Did anything surprising happen when you were creating patterns?

   - What was the most interesting pattern that was created?

   - What do you think you can say about the interconnections that you formed between the enemy (or enemies) in your game and the way that you placed the blocks?

   - How do you think the relationship between the enemy and the block placement might be related to the overall level of challenge in the game (or the overall function of the game)?

WHAT TO EXPECT

These ideas can be applied to both the whole-group discussion/individual reflection and to the "Playtester Feedback" handout.

Novice	Expert
• Preoccupied with number of enemies and places little emphasis on their movement • Places emphasis on only one aspect of enemy movement (e.g., speed) • Incorporates enemies, but restricts movement and/or location of them to a small area of the game space. Focuses on enemy movement in terms of placement and direction of travel while paying little to no attention to interaction between enemies and elements of game space (e.g., structuring movement via block placement)	• Shows the understanding that enemies can present a challenge beyond the sheer number of them present (i.e., via tactical creation of movement patterns) • Attends to two or more variables of enemy movement (i.e., speed, start direction, turn direction, and patrolling) to establish movement pattern in the game that presents an effective challenge • Establishes enemy movement patterns that effectively create challenges across the game space (with respect to the goal of the game) • Very attentive to interactions between enemies and the elements of the game space (e.g., structuring movement via block placement)

DESIGN CHALLENGE 5, PART 2

PLAYTESTER FEEDBACK

Playtester's name: _____   Game name: _____

PLAYTESTER'S NOTES	DESIGNER'S REFLECTION
Be sure to include both what you liked and enjoyed about the game (warm feedback), and what you think could be changed to make it even better (cool feedback). Warm feedback: Cool feedback:	Notes:
Below, circle a number in each category to give the game designer feedback on his or her game. **CHALLENGE** What was the level of challenge in the game? 1 2 3 4 5 Too easy Too hard **AESTHETICS** Does the visual and audio design support the game concept? 1 2 3 4 5 Does not support Fully supports **DESIGN** How would you rate the design of the game space? 1 2 3 4 5 Weak Fantastic **PACING** What do you think of the pacing of the game? 1 2 3 4 5 Too slow Too fast **STORY** Does the story fit well with the game? 1 2 3 4 5 Not too well Very well	Notes:

Total time: 125 minutes

OVERVIEW

The final challenge of the module will involve modeling a complex system both on paper and in a game. Youths will explore a predator-prey system and learn about how it works—what its components are, how they interconnect and how they ultimately shape the overall functioning of the system. If desired, the group can also begin to talk about how a predator-prey system stays in balance through a kind of feedback called *balancing feedback*.

PRODUCT

Youths will create a game that models the predator-prey relationship.

TARGETED SYSTEMS THINKING CONCEPTS

This challenge encourages youths to think about what they've learned about systems in the context of a different system: predator-prey. Youths also will use the modeling skills that they've begun to develop in earlier challenges to think about what a predator-prey relationship would look like in a game. As usual, youths will have to think about interconnections between components when designing their games. If desired, they also can be encouraged to think about how systems stay in balance through a form of feedback called *balancing feedback*.

PARTS

CREATE A GAME: PREDATOR AND PREY

In this Design Challenge, youths are asked to analyze the real-world system of a predator-prey relationship and to model such systems by making games in Gamestar Mechanic (G*M). In doing so, they are asked to think carefully about the components of the system that they're representing and how those components interconnect to help the system to reach its goal.

Time: 125 minutes

KEY DEFINITIONS

Identifying a system. Specifically, a *system* is a collection of two or more components and processes that interconnect to function as a whole. Speed and comfort in a car for example are created by the interactions of the car's parts and thus are "greater than the sum" of all separate parts of the car. The way a system works is not the result of a single part but is produced by the interaction among the components and/or individual agents within it. A key way to differentiate things that are systems from things that aren't is to consider whether the overall way something works in the world will change if you remove one part of it.

Identify the way a system is functioning. The function of a system describes the overall behavior of the system—what it is doing or where it's going over time. A system's function might emerge naturally based on interconnections among components, or it might be the result of an intentional design (in which case, we might also refer to the function of a system as its goal). Regardless, the function of a system is the result of the dynamics that occur among components' interconnected behaviors.

Distinguishing the goal of a system. The *goal* of the system is what it was intentionally designed to do. Sometimes this might be the same as the functioning of the system … other times the goal and the function are not aligned.

Identifying components. *Components* are the parts of a system that contribute to its functioning. Without being able to effectively identify the parts of a system, it's hard to understand how a system is actually working and how it might be changed.

Identifying behaviors. *Behaviors* are the specific actions or roles that a component of a system displays under various conditions. Being able to identify behaviors becomes important when we change systems, as often a component will look the same after the change but its behavior will be different.

Identifying interconnections. *Interconnections* are the different ways that a system's parts, or components, interact with each other through their behaviors, and through those interactions change the behaviors of other components.

Make systems visible. When we learn to "make the system visible"— whether modeling a system on the back of a napkin, through a computer simulation, a game, a picture, a diagram, a set of mathematical computations, or a story—we can use these representations to communicate about how things work. At their best, good pictures of systems help both the creator and the "reader" or "audience" to understand not only the parts of the system (the components), but also, how those components work together to produce a whole.

Balancing feedback loops. *Feedback loops* are circular, cause-and-effect processes that create stability by counteracting or dampening change. These processes keep a system at the desired state of equilibrium, the system goal. Usually, balancing feedback processes stabilize systems by limiting or preventing certain processes from happening. Having a sense of how balancing feedback loops operate can give a person a sense of what will make a system stable.

COMMON CORE STATE STANDARDS COVERED—ENGLISH LANGUAGE ARTS	NEXT GENERATION SCIENCE STANDARDS
• R.6–12.7	• 3–5-ETS1–1
• RI.7.3	• 3–5-ETS1–2
• RI.7.7	• 3–5-ETS1–3
• W.7.6	• MS-ETS1–1
• RST.6–8.7	• MS-ETS1–2
• RST.6–8.9	• MS-ETS1–3
• RST.11–12.9	• MS-ETS1–4
• SL.6–12.4	

MATERIALS OVERVIEW

- Digital projector
- Whiteboard or large paper
- Markers
- Pencils
- A set of video clips of different examples of predatory-prey relationships
- A simulation loaded to review with the group

HANDOUTS

- "Balancing Feedback Loops"
- "Modeling Predator-Prey"
- "Playtester Feedback"

OVERALL CHALLENGE PREPARATION

Select one or more video clips featuring examples of predatory-prey relationships. Video series such as *Blue Planet* or *Planet Earth* are excellent resources, and YouTube contains many short clips that youths can explore on their own. Plan to prescreen the material to ensure that nothing too graphic happens when predator meets prey.

One video that demonstrates the relationship between predator and prey can be found here:

videos.howstuffworks.com/discovery/28234-assignment -discovery-glow-worms-video.htm

A simulation modeling the relationship between wolves and deer can be found here:

www.sims.scienceinstruction.org/predprey/index.html

CREATE A GAME: PREDATOR AND PREY

In this part of the challenge, youths are asked to analyze the real-world system of a predator-prey relationship and to model such systems by making games in G*M. In so doing, they are asked to think carefully about the components of the system that they're representing and how those components interconnect to help the system to reach its goal.

Time: 125 minutes

STUFF TO HAVE HANDY

- A set of video clips of different examples of predatory-prey relationships
- A predator-prey simulation loaded to review with the group

HANDOUTS

- "Balancing Feedback Loops"
- "Modeling Predator-Prey"
- "Playtester Feedback"

RESEARCH: GETTING FAMILIAR WITH PREDATOR-PREY—40 MINUTES

Begin the meeting by showing the video clips that have been collected of different examples of predator-prey relationships. Note that most video clips show the relationship between a predator and a prey, but not necessarily the long-term relations that exist between the animals. Specifically, the videos suggest that the predator-prey relationship consists merely of two components: the predator and the prey. This will be a good starting point, to ensure that all youths have a vision of the predator-prey relationship actually looks like. However, to help youths think more deeply about the relationship, including what additional components are part of the system (what the prey eat, how often the predators eat, how quickly predators reproduce as opposed to prey), and about how these relationships are sustained over time (that is, the myriad interconnections between these components), it will be useful to review a simulation with the youths.

1. Choose one or two videos about the predator-prey relationship to watch. Then ask youths the following questions:

    •   What are the components of the system that you just observed?

    •   What behaviors does each component display?

    •   What are the interconnections between these components?

    •   Do you think there are other components of the system that weren't pictured? (For example, what does the prey animal eat? How many prey animals would each predator consume? How often would prey consumption occur? How about predator reproduction?).

2. Open the predator-prey simulation that you have prepared and review the parameters with the youths. Note that the number of wolves and deer are fixed initially, but they change over time. Allow youths to hypothesize about how different factors might affect the relationship between the predator and prey and then test out those hypotheses with the simulation. Ask the following questions:

- What additional components are part of this system that we didn't notice before?

- Is it possible for this system to get out of balance? Could there be many deer and no wolves? Many wolves but no deer? What would happen?

3. *Optional:* If you decide that you want to address the concept of balancing feedback with your youths, introduce that topic now. Explain that, when properly balanced, wolves and deer populations can stay relatively stable basically forever because there is a consistent relationship between the number of deer that the environment can support (i.e., only so much grass and trees) and the number of wolves that can live on deer. If too many wolves came into being, the deer population would decline, but ultimately the wolf population would decline as well (because they didn't have enough to eat when the deer population declines), which would allow the deer population to reestablish itself. This is called a *balanced system* because as one component increases (number of wolves), another component decreases (number of deer), which causes the number of wolves to go down, which allows the number of deer to go up. For an additional example, you can pass out the "Balancing Feedback Loops" handout and review it as a group.

4. Once everyone has a good grasp on predator-prey relationships, open G*M and introduce youths to the sprites that are particularly useful for predator-prey (i.e., the energy blocks, energy generator blocks, naviron nibbler, naviron chomper, naviron omnivore, naviron grazer, naviron gnasher, population counter, and energy meter). The youths can use any sprites that they choose, but they want to think about which sprites they are pairing up (predators that go after particular prey), what the prey need to survive, how they want to organize the space of the game, and how they can use the particular predator-prey blocks mentioned previously. Once you are sure that everyone has a grasp on the slightly different design challenge presented in modeling this system, youths can start to work independently on their games.

IMAGINE AND CREATE: MODELING PREDATOR-PREY IN G*M—40 MINUTES

In this next activity, youths will think about predator-prey systems and how to model aspects of that system within G*M.

1. Pass out the "Modeling Predator-Prey" handouts.

2. Ask youths to take some time to fill in the worksheet, paying particular attention to the interconnections that they are designing between the different sprites in the game, as well as the placement and type of blocks used. When youths appear to have a plan, encourage them to put it into action in G*M.

3. Using their worksheets as a reference, have the youths model aspects of predator-prey relationships in G*M by choosing appropriate avatars, enemies, and items, and making adjustments to the parameters of those sprites. The youths also can be challenged to design the space and background of the game based on the particular environment in which the animals they are modeling belong.

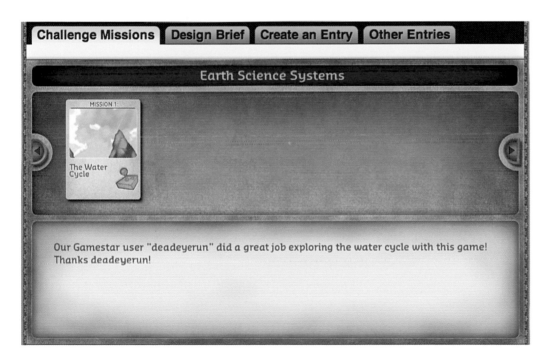

4. As in the previous Design Challenges, for the next activity to work, youths *must* have redeemed a special code within G*M that provides access to the Design Challenges in *Gaming the System*. Note that this only needs to be done once, so if they completed this step in an earlier Design Challenge, they can proceed directly to the next step. If this hasn't been done, direct them to follow this link: **gamestar mechanic.com/?activation=GAMINGTHESYSTEM**. They will be prompted to login (if they haven't already). They then click the Redeem button.

5. Have youths log in to G*M and click on "Workshop." Then have them find the "Earth Science Systems" Challenge. When they are ready to design, they should click on the "Create an Entry" tab. (See screenshot on p. 185.)

6. As youths are working, be sure to ask them how they're thinking about the design goal of the game—do they want the game to end or the system to function in a particular way (with either the predators or prey triumphing?), or are they interested in keeping the system in balance?

VOICES FROM THE FIELD

On one occasion, I had one of my youths give me feedback on a game I was designing. He first watched me go through the game on the big screen and made an evaluation on how challenging the play was, the aesthetics, the design, pacing, and story line. The youth evaluated my game, gave me minor feedback, changing the background for the aesthetics, and suggested I add a timer with 3 minutes on it. After I made the changes, I had the youth play the game to get the feel. After he had played the game for a little bit, I had him go in and edit the health of the avatar to 3 from 5 to make the game more challenging. He made the changes and played for a little bit, then revised his feedback and gave me some additional thoughts and critiques. I brought this youth up to the front of the room and we went through the process to be the example for the class on giving feedback on games.

—TRAVIS POWELL, OREGON WRITING PROJECT

PLAY, SHARE, AND REFLECT: PLAYTESTING OTHERS' GAMES—20 MINUTES

Professional game designers learn constantly from the feedback that their players give them on their games. In this activity, youths will get a twofold benefit from this practice as they explore each other's designs and learn what their peers think about their own.

1. Pair up youths and ask them to play each other's games for about 5 minutes.

2. When the 5 minutes are up, ask youths to fill out the "Playtester Feedback" handout. Encourage youths to provide detailed, constructive feedback, using the handout to organize their thinking.

3. After about 5 minutes of independent writing, ask the youths to take turns sharing their feedback. Be sure that youths are *not* just passing their forms to each other, but that each reviewer actually reads the feedback aloud so that the designer is able to listen and ask questions for clarification. Be sure to emphasize that *more* detail is better than *less* detail, and that all feedback should include both compliments (warm feedback) and suggestions for improvement (cool feedback).

ITERATE: REDESIGN IN G*M—15 MINUTES

Ask youths to revise their games based on playtester feedback.

SHARE: PREDATOR-PREY—10 MINUTES

The goal of this final whole-group discussion is to help youths reflect on the games that they have just designed and think about them in terms of the systems that they represent.

1. Either ask for volunteers or choose a couple of youths whose games are quite different from each other. Invite the youths to play their games for the entire group.

2. Ask the youths to explain how they decided which predator-prey sprites to use, which blocks to include, and how they thought about the interconnections among those elements as supporting the goal of the system (either to keep the predator-prey relations in balance or to throw it out of balance purposely). As they are presenting, encourage the youths to think about the following questions:

- Why did you choose a particular movement pattern? How did you decide (a) which sprite to use and (b) where in the game space to place that sprite?

- Did anything surprising happen when you played the game?

- What are some of the interconnections that you can observe in your game?

WHAT TO EXPECT

Novice	Expert
• Understands that components (such as avatar and enemy) have distinct behaviors • Understands how some behaviors directly interact • Struggles with the notion of "balance" in a system • Doesn't think about interactions among more than two components	• Has a sense of how components of the system interact and affect one another, and in particular, thinks about more than two components interacting • Can describe what it means for a system to be out of balance • Understands solutions to resolving situations when systems are out of balance • Recognizes that sometimes a small change to a component can make a significant impact on the overall behavior of the system (game-play experience)

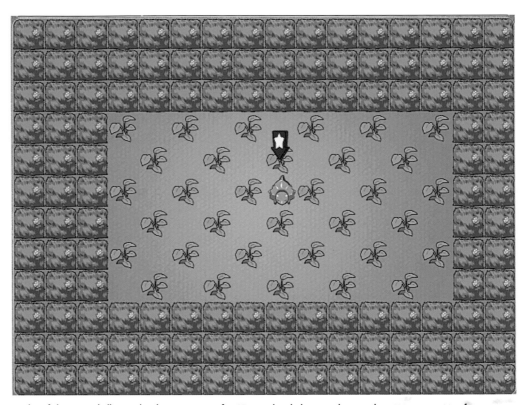

Level 1 of the game challenges the player to survive for 45 seconds, which is easy because there is no competition for resources. (Credit: *Dinosaur Sustainability* by Rhys)

Level 2 introduces a second predator — and suddenly competition for resources is fierce! (Credit: *Dinosaur Sustainability* by Rhys)

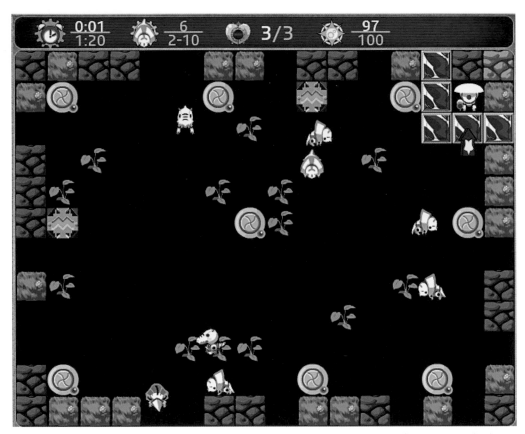

This game uses an energy generator to spawn new energy items (plants) to feed your avatar. But there are many other hungry creatures competing for similar resources. The design challenge in this game was to create the right balance of predators to prey to ensure that neither group becomes extinct. (Credit: *Extinction Predator-Prey* by Travis P)

DESIGN CHALLENGE 6: PREDATOR-PREY

BALANCING FEEDBACK LOOPS

Definition:

Circular, cause-and-effect processes that create stability by counteracting or dampening change.

These processes keep a system at the desired state of equilibrium, the system goal. Usually, balancing feedback processes stabilize systems by limiting or preventing certain processes from happening.

Examples:

- **Hunger:**

  Shannon is hungry, so she eats. When Shannon eats, her feeling of hunger decreases, which causes her to stop eating. Eventually, Shannon's body utilizes the energy from her food intake and will require more, causing her to be hungry again.

- **Flushing Toilet:**

  When you flush a toilet, the water level drops, which activates the mechanism in the back reservoir to fill with water. The back reservoir stops filling with water once the level returns to normal.

- **Itching and Scratching:**

  When your skin itches, you scratch it to relieve the itching feeling. Once the itching feeling subsides, you stop scratching until the itch returns.

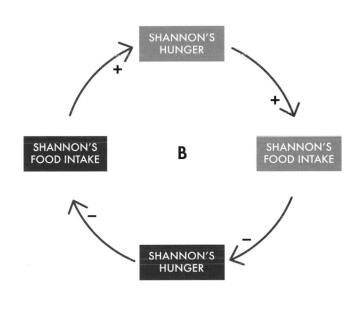

MODELING PREDATOR-PREY

DESIGN PLANS:

1. What predator-prey relationship do you plan to model?

2. How will you ensure that a player is able to understand the predator-prey relationship?

3. Which components will you use to represent the predator and the prey?

4. How do you want the predator and prey to move around in the space?

5. What is the goal of your game?

PLAYTESTER FEEDBACK

Playtester's name: _____   Game name: _____

PLAYTESTER'S NOTES	DESIGNER'S REFLECTION
Be sure to include both what you liked and enjoyed about the game (warm feedback), and what you think could be changed to make it even better (cool feedback).	Notes:
Warm feedback:	
Cool feedback:	

Below, circle a number in each category to give the game designer feedback on his or her game.	Notes.

CHALLENGE What was the level of challenge in the game?

1	2	3	4	5
Too easy				Too hard

AESTHETICS Does the visual and audio design support the game concept?

1	2	3	4	5
Does not support				Fully supports

DESIGN How would you rate the design of the game space?

1	2	3	4	5
Weak				Fantastic

PACING What do you think of the pacing of the game?

1	2	3	4	5
Too slow				Too fast

STORY Does the story fit well with the game?

1	2	3	4	5
Not too well				Very well

PLAYTESTER'S NOTES	DESIGNER'S REFLECTIONS
What was challenging about the game?	Notes:
What suggestions do you have to make the game more difficult?	Notes:

DELVING DEEPER INTO SYSTEMS THINKING

The significant problems we face cannot be solved at the same level of thinking we were at when we created them.

—Albert Einstein

We are caught in an inescapable network of mutuality, tied in a single garment of destiny. Whatever affects one directly affects all indirectly.

—Dr. Martin Luther King, Jr.

So what is systems thinking, and why is it important? With so little time to cover what seems like so much, why should systems thinking get a seat at the educational table? We find the answer in part by looking at the vast problems in the world around us, which range from environmental degradation to global financial meltdowns, growing inequality to ballooning costs of health care, and so many more issues. At their core, these difficulties are about systems, and all can be linked fundamentally to perspective: people have a tendency to look at things in terms of isolated parts instead of interdependent wholes. In short, to solve these complex problems, we need to view the world as a set of complex systems.

We believe that teaching systems thinking holds promise for supporting the development of a generation of young people who look at things differently, through "new lenses" that will allow them to effectively meet the challenges of a world that is more connected than ever. These lenses involve looking before leaping, an orientation toward understanding the big picture, and the approach of *interpreting* things differently rather than *doing* them differently. After all, change in the ways we *do* things naturally follows from a change in the way we *see* things. Rather than focusing on a narrow analysis of phenomena that we too often assume are standing still, a systems thinking approach always assumes that the world is in constant motion, and that in that world, nothing exists in isolation. So the systems thinker learns to focus on the dynamics that surround, shape, and are shaped by whatever it is that we want to understand, whether it be in the realm of science, sociology, economics, or English literature. Systems thinkers seek to understand the impact of their actions on the often tightly interconnected system of which they are a part.

WHAT MAKES A SYSTEMS THINKER DIFFERENT? IT'S ALL ABOUT PERSPECTIVE!

As mentioned previously, much of systems thinking deals with changing our perspectives on situations and adopting the kinds of perspectives that people aren't often taught. Specifically, several practices are engaged in regularly by someone acting from a systems thinking perspective:

- Looking at the world in terms of integrated and interdependent wholes, as opposed to isolated parts

- Knowing that most complex problems involve dynamic systems that are in motion, rather than static parts that stand still

- Viewing situations from multiple levels of perspective, focusing on the connections between events and the underlying patterns, systemic structures, and assumptions from which those events emerge

- Considering how a particular stakeholder's position within a system will affect his or her ideas and assumptions about a system's function and how it should operate

- Adjusting the sense of time—by expanding the range of time considered when looking at a problem, you can gain insights into how certain actions in a system might have delayed effects

- Identifying the various dynamics, especially circular ones in the form of feedback loops, which lead a system to function in a particular way and move in a particular direction

- Focusing on finding leverage points that can be used to make lasting changes, as opposed to falling back on short-term fixes

- Considering the unintended consequences of intervening in a system

Think about the difference between a person who is able to do the things on that list and one who cannot. In an interconnected world, young people who are trained as systems thinkers have a powerful way of understanding, participating in, and changing the structures that affect their lives and those of people they care about.

WHAT MAKES A SYSTEM A SYSTEM?

A system isn't just a whole bunch of stuff that happens to be lumped together geographically or topically. It's not limited to what we usually call *systems* in our daily lives, such as when we refer to our education or healthcare systems, a computer system, or a heating system in a building (though these definitely *are* systems!). Systems have particular qualities, and knowing and being able to identify them is a key part of being able to look at things systemically.

Linda Booth Sweeney, a leader in the field of systems thinking, likes to talk about the difference between systems and heaps (Sweeney 2001). Both, she says, contain lots of "stuff," or parts. But a heap won't be changed much if you take away some of its parts. Think of a pile of laundry. Add or take away a couple of shirts or a towel, and you still have a pile of laundry—not really a substantive change. Now think of a washing machine. Try taking off the door handle, adding a slot for detergent that doesn't connect to the rest of the machine, or changing the amount of electricity that feeds into the machine. Good luck getting socks clean! That pile of laundry is a heap, where adding and taking away things won't really affect the pile very much (if at all) in terms of how it functions in the world. But a washing machine is a system—we can't just add, take away, or change elements willy-nilly since these often are interconnected in specific ways, often feeding back on one another, and have specific roles or behaviors that allow the system to function in a particular way.

Here's one definition of system that we like to use: A *system* is a collection of interacting *components* that interact to *function* as a whole, where the whole is always greater than the sum of its parts. If you change one component, the whole functions differently. Although this may appear to be relatively straightforward on the surface, identifying the components of a system requires understanding how a system actually works. There are many things that might occur around a system that does not actually affect its overall behavior. For example, in the video games that youths design in *Gaming the System*, they can select different backgrounds for their games. Although these decisions must be made for every game design, and although it can be argued that they affect the aesthetic experience of the game, the background is not a component of the overall function of the system (i.e., the game) as a whole. With that in mind, when we ask youths to consider the components of a system, we are asking them to discriminate between central and peripheral components of their systems. In *Gaming the System*, youths deal with a range of components (which in the game are called *sprites*) such as blocks, avatars, enemies, time, points, and goals. More broadly, when applying systems thinking to the way that we look at different parts of a world, a key element of determining what a system is involves figuring out what is part of the system and what isn't. Often, problems in the world are misunderstood because the people looking at them are either missing some important components or including ones that actually aren't that important.

All of these components are set up in a particular way, interacting in relation to one another, which is called a system's *structure*. The structure of a system determines the specific *behaviors* of different parts and the specific *system dynamics* that result from the interactions among the components. For example, the components that we've mentioned behave in particular ways depending on how they're used. The behavior of a block can be to create a path for the avatar, and it also potentially influences how enemies move within a game. In addition, blocks can have specialized behaviors, such as being permeable, giving damage, or serving as space warps. The behavior of enemies is quite varied: their speed, direction, movement pattern, health, and damage can all be changed, and these behaviors can interact and sometimes be shaped by other components. Likewise, the behavior of avatars is also quite varied: their speed, health, and damage all can be changed. This may seem straightforward, but understanding the behavior (potential and realized) of a particular component allows someone to be able to consider how behaviors of components interconnect and how they can design and intervene in systems.

A SYSTEM'S GOAL, PURPOSE, AND FUNCTION: NOT ALL ARE CREATED EQUAL

One of the tricky elements of systems is the fact that there's often a difference between the way that a system is *actually* working (its *function*) and how we *want* it to work (its *goal*). This is why so many of us try to intervene in existing systems—because they're not working well (or maybe they're working well for some, but not for all).

There are many cases where a system is functioning exactly as it was intended to by someone designing or intervening in it. Let's take the example of a game. A game can be considered a system because how the game is played and how the game play unfolds are the results of multiple interactions among different components. The *function* of the system (the experience of playing the game) might be really difficult—and a designer might have meant it to be so (her *goal* might have been to create a difficult game). On the other hand, sometimes the overall function of a system is *at odds* with the intended goal that someone has for the system. For instance, from one perspective, the *goal* or purpose of a car is to take someone from point A to point B; but when the car's transmission gives out, the car will not *function* as a system to meet that goal. The game design module generally encourages students to think about how systems are functioning by talking about the overall game play experience. For example, a system end point (the system function) might be a game that is really challenging—or really easy.

It's important to be able to reflect not only on how a system might be functioning currently, but also on how a designer might have intended it to operate (or intended to change it). A given system might have multiple goals that are at play simultaneously, but come into conflict. The person who designed the washing machine has a pretty straightforward goal: get clothing clean (without destroying it in the process). Many systems are more complex than a washing machine, however, and have a less straight forward purpose. For example, the educational system has many components (e.g., teachers, youths, school buildings, assessments, and educational standards), all of which, presumably, are meant to work together in order to . . . do what? Well, that question is actually a matter of some dispute. Like many other systems, such as health care, social services, economies, businesses, and communities, the educational system has more than one person who acts as a "designer"—that is, there are multiple actors bringing varying goals and purposes to the design of a given system and contributing to the way that it is configured.

In the case of the educational system, some people believe that the purpose of being educated is to develop a population that is well prepared to engage in the project of democracy (this was Thomas Jefferson's view), while others see its purpose as preparing young people to compete in the global economy. These are only two possible goals, and while there might be some overlap of goals, we probably can agree that an educational system that aims at only one of the goals likely would look different from one that aims at the other. Knowing that any given system can have different stakeholders working toward different goals sometimes can help us understand why a system is not functioning as well as it could be. After all, not all goals are compatible.

Often, though, the way that systems actually operate is more organic than intentional. Many environmental issues involving the interaction of human behavior with natural ecosystems can be described as the result of systems whose functions are completely unintended. Global warming, for instance, results from the interaction of many components (human fossil fuel emissions, carbon dioxide's capacity to retain heat, the particular makeup of the Earth's atmosphere that captures certain gases, etc.), which all create a system that functions to increase global climate over time. Obviously, this was not anyone's intention, but it points to the fact that while many systems are designed and have intended goals or consequences (like that washing machine), others have their own logic and function that is driven by an emergent system structure (like economies and ecosystems).

SYSTEM STRUCTURE

The way that a system's components are set up in relation to one another, known as the *system structure,* is another important factor in understanding systems. On their own, components don't do very much. However, once they're connected to one another, they start to take on specific behaviors and roles within a system. These behaviors aren't a given, though; they depend on the way that the system is structured. For instance, if I take apart a car, lay out all the parts, and then put them back together in a different way, it's unlikely that the car will work the way that it did before or that the parts will exhibit their original behaviors. The relationships between the car parts are contingent on how they're structured.

In *Gaming the System*, youths often think that the way to make a game more difficult is to add more enemies. This is a simple causal explanation: enemies are bad, so adding more of them would make the game harder. Instead, with experience, youths begin to understand that it isn't necessarily true that adding more enemies makes the game more difficult, and it is most certainly true that there are many other ways to make the game more difficult besides simply adding enemies. As youths get more sophisticated in their thinking, they begin to realize that the change has to be considered in light of the way the components of the game are structured. In the process of investigating these inter-connections, youth often discover that systems work in ways that are counterintuitive. For example, they might find that making a small change (such as moving a block or changing the speed of an enemy) might have a significant impact on the function of the game (making it much more challenging or much easier). Youths also might discover that there is no central "control" in the system telling the components what to do; rather, they learn that the ultimate behavior of the system is driven by the interconnections among the components.

Understanding this idea requires attending to the *interconnections* among compo-nents. Behaviors are generally meaningful only when they interact with each other; when that occurs, contact with another component often *affects* or *changes* the behavior of the first component. This is the way that systems ultimately function—rather than component A affecting component B, which then affects component C, interconnections describe some kind of recursiveness or feedback among the components: When compo-nent A affects component B, that affects both component A and component C, and so on. In Gamestar Mechanic (G*M), myriad components interconnect to create a game that functions in a way that's difficult or easy for the player. The behavior of your avatar can interconnect with the behavior of an enemy to influence the progress of the game. For example, if an avatar has a low health level and is easy to kill, and the enemy can create a lot of damage, it creates a situation where the enemy will kill the avatar very quickly, making the game more difficult. However, there are other components of the game that can affect the way that that interconnection takes place. For example, if there are very few blocks in the game, which makes it relatively easy for the avatar to avoid the enemy, the enemy's ability to do damage becomes insignificant. Likewise, if the goal block is very close to the starting point (in other words, winning the game involves traveling only a very short distance), then again, the enemy's capacity for mayhem and the avatar's weakness are unimportant. Understanding and predicting interconnections lie at the heart of systems thinking because it is the interconnections that ultimately drive the way a system behaves.

LEVERAGE POINTS: INTERVENING AND CHANGING SYSTEMS

Understanding how systems work is all well and good, but if that insight isn't used to actually do something in the world, then it's just an academic exercise. Our vision of teaching systems thinking is rooted in the idea that young people eventually will become designers of new systems and redesigners of the systems that they inherit from us, and so some of the core ideas that we focus on are those related to how to change and intervene in systems.

When we think about changing systems, we think about *leverage points*. What makes a leverage point unique and powerful is that it's a place within a system where "a small change in one thing can produce big changes in everything," as activist and systems theorist Donella Meadows says. In a now-foundational book in the systems thinking world called *Leverage Points: Places to Intervene in a System* (1999), Meadows outlines different ways we can think about possible leverage points that range from less effective (e.g., changing the amount of "stuff" associated with certain parts of a system or changes to the structures that handle the movement of this "stuff") to more effective (e.g., changing the rules that govern a system, or better yet, the mindset that leads to things like rules, goals, and structure). While we won't go through all of the leverage points that Meadows outlined, we want to stress that focusing on leverage points isn't like generating any old solution to a problem; they are designed not only to take into account the structures of a system, but also take advantage of these structures so that a little change can go a long way.

In a wonderful example of leverage points at work, Meadows shares the story of the Toxic Release Inventory, which required every factory that released air pollutants to document and report data on these pollutants publicly. When the inventory was instituted in 1986 by the US government, toxic emissions were reduced dramatically. The inventory didn't levy fines or make the process of releasing these chemicals into the air illegal—it simply made the information public. By 1990, toxic emissions in the United

States dropped by 40 percent. Factory owners did not want to be known publicly as polluters, so they changed their practices. The availability of information to different stakeholders within a system (in this case, citizens) changed the way that this system operated. The Toxic Release Inventory targeted a leverage point: It didn't aim to remake the whole system to prevent pollution; rather, it just added one small part that wasn't there before. It was a minor change, but it had a big effect.

In *Gaming the System*, students play and experiment with ways to change games that have the most significant impact. For example, in some games, simply changing the time allotted for game play can make it significantly more difficult. Suddenly, other components, such as the speed of the avatar, the location of the blocks, the number of tasks that need to be completed before reaching the goal, and the number of enemies that need to be avoided or destroyed, have significant effects on a player's overall success. If there is no time limit or a long time limit, a player has the privilege of waiting for enemies to pass or taking inefficient routes to accomplish particular tasks. Shortening the time limit significantly affects the importance of these other component behaviors, and therefore the overall function (or difficulty) of the game.

GLOSSARY OF KEY TERMS

Identifying a system.   Identifying a system and distinguishing it from other kinds of things that aren't systems. Specifically, a system is a collection of two or more components and processes that interconnect to function as a whole. Speed and comfort in a car for example are created by the interactions of the car's parts and thus are "greater than the sum" of all separate parts of the car. The way a system works is not the result of a single part but is produced by the interaction among the components and/or individual agents within it. A key way to differentiate things that are systems from things that aren't is to consider whether the overall way something works in the world will change if you remove one part of it.

Identify the way a system is functioning.   The function of a system describes the overall behavior of the system—what it is doing or where it's going over time. A system's function might emerge naturally based on interconnections among components, or it might be the result of an intentional design (in which case, we might also refer to the function of a system as its goal). Regardless, the function of a system is the result of the dynamics that occur among components' interconnected behaviors. For example, components in a game might be set up in a way that makes the game unplayable, even if a designer wants it to be fun. Or, it might be playable, but really hard.

Distinguishing the goal of a system. The goal of the system is what a system that was intentionally designed is intended to do. Sometimes this might be the same as the functioning of the system ... other times the goal and the function are not aligned. A given system might have multiple goals or purposes that are at play simultaneously and come into conflict. Being able to understand system purpose or goal gives a sense of the ideal state of a system from a particular perspective. The goal of a game might be to create an experience that is challenging and enjoyable at the same time (though different game designers can have different goals!).

Identifying components. Components are the parts of a system that contribute to its functioning. Components have certain qualities and/or behaviors that determine how they interconnect with other components, as well as define their role in the system. Without being able to effectively identify the parts of a system, it's hard to understand how a system is actually functioning and how it might be changed. A game can be made of power ups, enemies, the game space, the player's avatar, as well as other components. For example, all sprites in Gamestar Mechanic are components with unique behaviors. Some sprites, like the timer, control time; other sprites, like enemies, cause damage to avatar sprites.

Identifying behaviors. Behaviors are the specific actions or roles that a component of a system displays under various conditions. Being able to identify behaviors becomes important when we change systems, as often a component will look the same after the change, but its behavior will be different. For example, in a game the behavior of the enemy might be that it can only move in one direction.

Identifying interconnections. Interconnections are the different ways that a system's parts, or components, interact with each other through their behaviors, and through those interactions, change the behaviors of other components.

Perceiving dynamics. Perceiving a system's dynamics involves looking at a higher level at how the system works. Dynamics in a system are often characterized by circles—patterns that "feed back" on one another. These are called feedback loops.

Considering the role of system structure. Understanding how a system's components are set up in relation to one another gives insight into the behavior of a component. A system's structure affects the behaviors of its components and the overall dynamics and functioning of a system. For instance, how a city's highway system is structured affects overall traffic patterns and car movement within it. Being able to see a system's structure gives insights into the mechanisms and relationships that are at the core of a system, which can be leveraged to create systemic changes. For example, if an enemy sprite turns right every time it encounters a block, the structure of the game space will determine the enemy's pattern of movement.

Make systems visible. When we learn to "make the system visible"—whether modeling a system on the back of a napkin, through a computer simulation, a game, a picture, a diagram, a set of mathematical computations, or a story—we can use these representations to communicate about how things work. At their best, good pictures of systems help both the creator and the "reader" or "audience" to understand not only the parts of the system (the components), but also, how those components work together to produce a whole. For example, a map is a visual model of a certain area. Different maps will include or leave out different details about that area, depending on their purpose. A map of New York City that's used to navigate its subway system looks very different from a map of New York City that's used to navigate its streets by car. Game designers often model systems in the games they design, making choices about what parts of the model to include and what parts to leave out.

Designing a system. Systems can be created through engaging in an iterative design process, one that entails iterative cycles of feedback, troubleshooting, and testing. One of the most effective means of developing systems thinking is to regularly create and iterate on the design of systems, and doing so in a way that creates opportunities for students to think about generic systems models that apply across multiple domains and settings.

Balancing feedback loops. Feedback loops are circular, cause-and-effect processes that create stability by counteracting or dampening change. These processes keep a system at the desired state of equilibrium, the system goal. Usually, balancing feedback processes stabilize systems by limiting or preventing certain processes from happening. Having a sense of how balancing feedback loops operate can give a person a sense of what will make a system stable.

ADDITIONAL GAME DESIGN RESOURCES

GAME DESIGN PLATFORMS

Adventure Game Studio   Adventure Game Studio is a free software development tool that is primarily used to create graphical adventure games. It is aimed at intermediate-level game designers and combines an integrated development environment (IDE) for setting up most aspects of the game with a scripting language to process the game logic.

www.adventuregamestudio.co.uk

Level: Intermediate to advanced

ARIS   ARIS is a user-friendly, open-source platform for creating and playing mobile games, tours, and interactive stories. Using global positioning systems (GPS) and quick response (QR) codes, ARIS players experience a hybrid world of virtual interactive characters, items, and media placed in physical space.

arisgames.org

Level: Beginner +

GameMaker   GameMaker is designed to allow its users to develop computer games easily, without having to learn a complex programming language such as C++ or Java. GameMaker's primary development interface uses a drag-and-drop system, allowing users unfamiliar with traditional programming to intuitively create games by visually organizing icons on the screen.

www.yoyogames.com

Level: Intermediate to advanced

Kodu   Kodu is a visual programming language made specifically for creating games. It lets kids create games on the PC and Xbox via a simple visual programming language, and it can be used to teach creativity, problem solving, storytelling, and programming. Kodu for the PC is available to download for free and can be purchased for the Xbox.

www.kodugamelab.com

Level: Intermediate to advanced

7scenes   7scenes is a mobile storytelling platform that provides youths with tools to develop location-based tours and games for smart phones. It is a complete suite with an authoring toolkit, apps for iPhone and Android, a web platform, and admin tools.

7scenes.com

Level: Beginner +

LEVEL DESIGN PLATFORMS

LittleBigPlanet 1 or 2   LittleBigPlanet is a puzzle platformer video game for Sony PlayStation 3 (PS3) that has a "create" mode that enables anyone to build and customize a 3-D platformer game quickly.

www.littlebigplanet.com

Level: Beginner +

Minecraft   Minecraft is an online game focused on creativity and building, which allows players to build constructions out of textured cubes in 3-D. Minecraft is the collaboration of a small team of educators and programmers from the United States and Finland who are working with Mojang AB of Sweden, the creators of Minecraft, to make the game affordable and accessible to schools everywhere. They have created a suite of tools designed specifically for use in classrooms.

minecraftedu.com

Level: Beginner +

Portal 2 Puzzle Maker   The Puzzle Maker (also known as Puzzle Creator or Editor) is an in-game puzzle editor for Portal 2 that allows the creation, testing, and publishing (to Steam Workshop) of custom single-player test chambers.

www.thinkwithportals.com

Level: Beginner +

Super Scribblenauts   Super Scribblenauts is a puzzle game for the Nintendo DS. The object of the game is help a character named Max to solve puzzles; players do so by writing or typing words to create objects, which can be used to solve the puzzle. The game includes a level editor that gives players the power to create their own puzzles.

en.wikipedia.org/wiki/Super_Scribblenauts

Level: Beginner +

GAME ENGINES

Torque Game Builder   Torque 2D is a powerful and easy to use 2-D game engine. With its intuitive and powerful editor, anyone can jump into game creation with little or no prior programming or game development knowledge.

www.garagegames.com/products/torque-2d

Level: Beginner +

Unity 3D   Unity 3D is a game development tool that has been designed to let you focus on creating amazing games. Unity consists of both an editor for developing and designing content and a game engine for executing the final product.

www.unity3d.com

Level: Intermediate to advanced

XNA Game Studio   XNA Game Studio is an IDE that includes tools and code development libraries that hobbyists, students, and other nonprofessionals can use to create computer games for Microsoft Windows and Xbox 360.

Level: Intermediate to advanced

GAME DESIGN READING

"THE GAME BEGINS WITH AN IDEA"

The Art of Game Design, chapter 6
Jesse Schell

"THE GAME IMPROVES THROUGH ITERATION"

The Art of Game Design, chapter 7
Jesse Schell

"PLAYTESTING"

Game Design Workshop, chapter 9
Tracy Fullerton

"HOW TO PROTOTYPE A GAME IN UNDER 7 DAYS"

Shalin Shodhan, Matt Kucic, Kyle Gray, and Kyle Gabler

> www.gamasutra.com/view/feature/2438/how_to_prototype_a
> _game_in_under_7_.php

IAN SCHREIBER ONLINE GAME DESIGN CONCEPTS:

For those interested in learning more about game design, Ian Schreiber is a professor who decided to experiment with creating a blog-based, online game design course. Even though the course is over, all the posts are still on the web, and there's a lot of great information there.

Here's the first lesson if you want to give it a try:

> gamedesignconcepts.wordpress.com/2009/06/29/level-1
> -overview-what-is-a-game

GAMING THE SYSTEM ASSESSMENT

Name: _____ Date: _____

1. What is the relationship among the following three things? You can explain your answer in words or pictures.

(a) studying, (b) grades, and (c) interest in the subject matter.

Based on your answer, what do you think would happen to studying and grades if your interest in the subject matter went *down?*

2. Think about the game of Musical Chairs. Identify the components of the game and how those components interconnect to affect the overall goal of the game.

What would happen if you removed one of the components of the game of Musical Chairs?

3. Carla and Jordan are having an argument about what will make the game shown here more challenging:

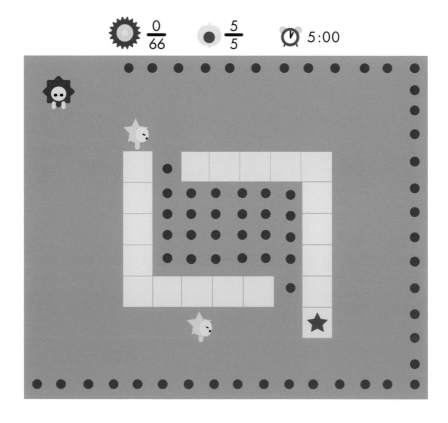

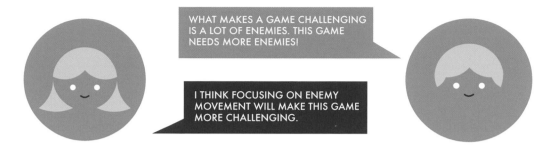

WHAT MAKES A GAME CHALLENGING IS A LOT OF ENEMIES. THIS GAME NEEDS MORE ENEMIES!

I THINK FOCUSING ON ENEMY MOVEMENT WILL MAKE THIS GAME MORE CHALLENGING.

Explain whether Carla is right or whether Jordan is right, and why.

What are some other ways that you could make this game challenging? Please explain.

4. What is the relationship between the amount of grass that is growing in a field, the number of rabbits who live in the area (rabbits eat grass), and the number of wolves in the area (wolves eat rabbits). Explain your answer in either words or pictures.

If someone decided to kill all the wolves, what would happen to the rabbits and the grass?

5. Here is a game that Jordan created. He is having trouble beating the game so is not yet allowed to publish it to Game Alley. Every time he plays, he loses after colliding with enemies twice. How could you adjust Jordan's game so that he has a better chance to collect all the coins and win? Explain your answer in words.

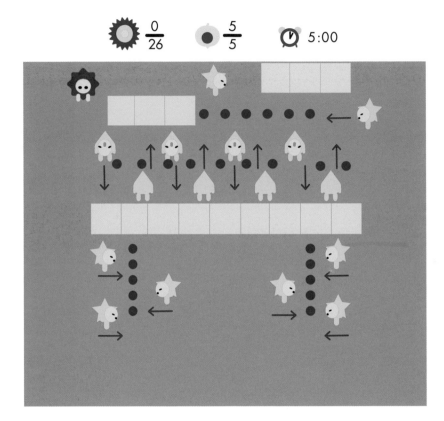

6. Carla suggested that Jordan remove some of the blocks to open up the game space a bit more. This is a diagram of the game based on Carla's suggestions. How do you think this will affect the game? Explain your answer in words.

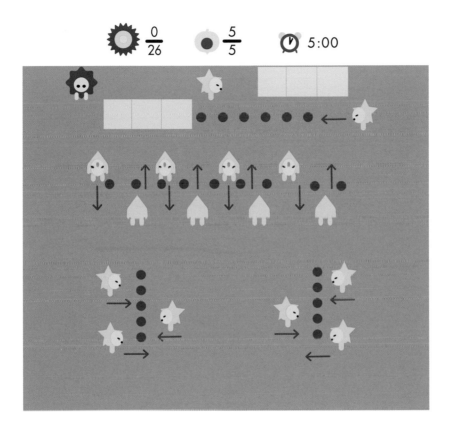

SYSTEMS THINKING CONCEPT CARDS: GAMING THE SYSTEM

The following cards have been included for you to use any way that works well in your setting, such as printing a set for each youth, creating a classroom deck to store in a resource center, or even using them as game cards for a whole-group games or activities (like Jeopardy!, Flyswatter, Baseball, and so on).

01.
IDENTIFYING A SYSTEM

Identifying a system and distinguishing it from other kinds of things that aren't systems. Specifically, a system is a collection of two or more components and processes that interconnect to function as a whole. Speed and comfort in a car for example are created by the interactions of the car's parts and thus are "greater than the sum" of all separate parts of the car. The way a system works is not the result of a single part but is produced by the interaction among the components and/or individual agents within it. A key way to differentiate things that are systems from things that aren't is to consider whether the overall way something works in the world will change if you remove one part of it.

02.
IDENTIFY THE WAY A
SYSTEM IS FUNCTIONING

The function of a system describes the overall behavior of the system–what it is doing or where it's going over time. A system's function might emerge naturally based on interconnections among components, or it might be the result of an intentional design (in which case, we might also refer to the function of a system as its goal). Regardless, the function of a system is the result of the dynamics that occur among components' interconnected behaviors.

03.
DISTINGUISHING THE GOAL
OF A SYSTEM

The goal of the system is what a system that was intentionally designed is intended to do. Sometimes this might be the same as the functioning of the system... other times the goal and the function are not aligned. A given system might have multiple goals or purposes that are at play simultaneously, and come into conflict. Being able to understand system purpose or goal gives a sense of the ideal state of a system from a particular perspective.

04.
IDENTIFYING COMPONENTS

Identifying the parts of a system that contribute to its functioning. Components have certain qualities and/or behaviors that determine how they interconnect with other components, as well as define their role in the system. Without being able to effectively identify the parts of a system, it's hard to understand how a system is actually functioning and how it might be changed.

05.
IDENTIFYING BEHAVIORS

Identifying the specific actions, roles, or behaviors that a component of a system displays under various conditions. Being able to identify behaviors becomes important when we change systems, as often a component will look the same after the change, but its behavior will be different.

06.
IDENTIFYING INTERCONNECTIONS

Identifying the different ways that a system's parts, or components, interact with each other through their behaviors, and through those interactions, change the behaviors of other components.

07.
PERCEIVING DYNAMICS

Perceiving a system's dynamics involves looking at a higher level at how the system works. Dynamics in a system are often characterized by circles–patterns that feed back on another. These are called feedback loops. Understanding dynamics gives insights into the mechanisms and relationships that are at the core of a system and can be leveraged to create systemic changes.

08.
CONSIDERING THE ROLE OF
SYSTEM STRUCTURE

Understanding how a system's components are set up in relation to one another gives insight into the behavior of a component. A system's structure affects the behaviors of its components and the overall dynamics and functioning of a system. For instance, how a city's highway system is structured affects overall traffic patterns and car movement within it. Being able to see a system's structure gives insights into the mechanisms and relationships that are at the core of a system, which can be leveraged to create systemic changes.

09.
MAKE SYSTEMS VISIBLE

When we learn to "make the system visible" – whether modeling a system on the back of a napkin, through a computer simulation, a game, a picture, a diagram, a set of mathematical computations, or a story—we can use these representations to communicate about how things work. At their best, good pictures of systems help both the creator and the "reader" or "audience" to understand not only the parts of the system (the components), but also, how those components work together to produce a whole.

10.
SYSTEMS DIAGRAM

Is a diagram used to visualize the dynamics that occur between components in a system, intended to capture how the variables interrelate. One way of diagramming a feedback loop uses an "R" with a clockwise arrow around it to indicate a reinforcing feedback loop. A "B" with a counterclockwise arrow around it would indicate a balancing feedback loop, which "counters" something in a system. The plus sign indicates an increase in that amount of a component in a system, and a minus sign indicates a decrease in the amount of a component in a system. There are other ways to create systems diagrams, but the most important thing about a good systems diagram is that it not only shows the components in a system, but is able to show the relationships between the components through the arrows, symbols, and text.

11.
FEEDBACK LOOPS

Are relationships between two or more components of a system, where actions by these components interact in a circular fashion – something that component A does effects component B, which then circles back and effects component A. There are two types of feedback loops, Balancing and Reinforcing.

12.
REINFORCING FEEDBACK LOOPS

Relationships where two or more components of a system cause each other to increase, such as in escalation cycles, or decrease, such in resource drain cycles, in a way that's "out of control" or creates a "snowball effect". Reinforcing loops encourage a system to reproduce certain behaviors, though these behaviors always "exhaust" themselves after the resources fueling the growth or diminishment run out. This is also called "limits to growth". There are two types of reinforcing feedback loops: "vicious" cycles and "virtuous" cycles.

13.
VICIOUS CYCLES

Reinforcing feedback loops that cause a negative outcome in terms of the perceived goal of the system. One thing to keep in mind is that the same thing might be a vicious cycle to one person, but a virtuous cycle for another person who has different goals.

14.
VIRTUOUS CYCLES

Reinforcing feedback loops that cause a positive outcome in terms the perceived goal of the system. One thing to keep in mind is that the same thing might be a virtuous cycle to one person, but a vicious cycle for another person who has different goals.

15.
BALANCING FEEDBACK LOOPS

Relationships where two or more elements of a system keep each other in balance, with one (or more) elements leading to increase, and one (or more) elements leading to decrease. These processes keep a system at the desired state of equilibrium, the system goal. Usually, balancing feedback processes stabilize systems by limiting or preventing certain processes from happening. Having a sense of how balancing feedback loops operate can give a person a sense of what will make a system stable.

16.
STOCKS & FLOWS

Stocks are an accumulated amount of something within a system (like money in a bank account, fish in a pond, trees in a forest, or jobs in an economy), and flows are the rate at which stocks in a system change either through increasing or decreasing (money comes in and out of a bank account due to wages paid, interest, and purchases. Fish come in and out of a pond due to birth rates, death rates, and fishing rates, etc.). Stocks are always nouns; they're the "stuff" of systems, while flows are always verbs; they're the "movement" of systems. Understanding Stocks and Flows gives someone an insight into how different parts of the system change over time.

17.
LIMITED RESOURCES

In any system, it is important to understand which resources are finite, ones that will run out at a certain point. Keeping in mind which resources are limited helps people make decisions about how best to maximize resources.

18.
NESTED SYSTEMS

Systems that are a smaller part of other systems. Almost all systems are nested within larger systems. With nested systems, a larger system will affect the way that a subsystem behaves, and the subsystem will affect the way that the larger system behaves. Having a sense of nested systems helps people keep an eye on how systems interconnect and are always part of bigger pictures.

19.
DYNAMIC EQUILIBRIUM

A state in which stocks and flows are balanced so the system is not varying widely, but still has internal dynamic processes that are continually in flux even though the system is stable overall. For example: in economics dynamic equilibrium might be used to talk about the constant flux of money movement in otherwise stable markets; in ecology, a population of organisms stabilizes when birth rate and death rate are in balance.

20.
DESIGNING A SYSTEM

Creating a system through engaging in an iterative design process, one that entails iterative cycles of feedback, troubleshooting and testing. One of the most effective means of developing systems thinking is to regularly create and iterate on the design of systems, and doing so in a way that creates opportunities for students to think about generic systems models that apply across multiple domains and settings.

21.
FIXES THAT FAIL

Any kind of solution to a problem that fixes the problem temporarily but fails fix it in the long term, and might even make it worse over time. Fixes that Fail are often put in place quickly, usually without much reflection on what consequences they'll have for the system. They're important to see since they're often the ways that people respond to problems in a system.

22.
LEVERAGE POINTS

Particular places within a system where a small shift in one thing can produce big changes in everything. Leverage points are difficult to find because they often lie far away from either the problem or the obvious solution. It is because of the multitude of cause and effect relationships, feedback loops and system structures that a seemingly small change can be amplified, often in unexpected ways. Not every place in a system is a leverage point – sometimes changing one thing in a system will just have small effects that aren't felt throughout the system. Leverage points are important since they let us know where to focus our energies when we try to change systems.

23.
UNINTENDED CONSEQUENCES

The unexpected result of an action taken in a system that the actor taking that original action did not want to happen. Unintended Consequences are often the result of fixes that fail or someone aiming to find a leverage point in a system but not considering long-term implications to those actions — someone failed to keep in mind time horizons. Having a good sense of potential unintended consequences means that someone will carefully consider before too hastily intervening in a system.

SYSTEMS THINKING CONCEPT CARDS:
GAMING THE SYSYTEM

24.

CONSIDERING HOW MENTAL
MODELS SHAPE ACTION IN A SYSTEM

The ability to consider the assumptions, ideas, and intentions that a given actor might have in relation to a system, and how these affect that actor's behavior within the system. Mental models are often correct about what components are included in a system, but frequently draw wrong conclusions about a system's overall behavior.

SYSTEMS THINKING CONCEPT CARDS:
GAMING THE SYSYTEM

25.

LOOKING AT A SYSTEM
FROM MULTIPLE PERSPECTIVES

The ability to understand that different actors in a system will have different mental models of the system and consider each of these perspectives when engaging in action within a system. This is also called "thinking across the table."

SYSTEMS THINKING CONCEPT CARDS:
GAMING THE SYSYTEM

26.

CONSIDERING MULTIPLE LEVELS
OF PERSPECTIVE

The ability to move fluidly between different levels of perspective within a system, from events, to patterns to system structures, to mental models. The most visible level of systems are events, visible instances of elements interacting in a system. Using the metaphor of a system as an iceberg, events are "above the waterline" – they're easy to see. When we start to think "below the waterline," we start to see three other levels of perspective: patterns (recurring sets of events), structures (ways the elements are set up in a system which give rise to regular patterns), and mental models (which shape systems structures). Switching between different levels of perspective when looking at a system deepens understanding of how a system operates.

SYSTEMS THINKING CONCEPT CARDS:
GAMING THE SYSYTEM

27.

TIME DELAYS

Are the time lag between an action in a system and the evidence of its effects. For example, there's a long delay between the point when you plant a seed in the ground and the appearance of a fruit-bearing tree.

SYSTEMS THINKING CONCEPT CARDS:
GAMING THE SYSYTEM

28.

TIME HORIZONS

Are the overall period of time that you look at something in order to understand it. For example, if we only look a complex system like an economy for a short period of time, we might misunderstand how it's behaving and miss the effects of actions taken far into the past.

SYSTEMS THINKING CONCEPT CARDS: GAMING THE SYSTEM

UNDERSTANDING SYSTEMS:
DIGITAL DESIGN FOR A COMPLEX WORLD

GAMING THE SYSTEM CHALLENGE CARDS

LEVELS
- ⬤ EASY
- ✦ MEDIUM
- ✺ HARD
- ❋ HARDCORE

OVERVIEW

Game design challenge cards offer a series of jumping off points for the creation of digital or non-digital games.

The cards in this deck allow budding game designers of all levels to design games inspired by simple challenges. Challenges are rated from easy to hardcore and come with some hints to help get things started.

Remember—all games are systems that change over time, so think DYNAMIC!

GAMING THE SYSTEM CHALLENGE CARDS	GAMING THE SYSTEM CHALLENGE CARDS	GAMING THE SYSTEM CHALLENGE CARDS

01 ROOM WITH A VIEW

LEVEL

EASY

Create a game made of a room with a view.

EXPLANATION

Games can include both interior and exterior spaces. The *Legend Of Zelda* is a great example, as is *Animal Crossing*.

HINTS

Try creating a series of rooms that lead to a window. Customize each room by using different kinds of blocks and enemies. Think about the different attributes you can give each space to distinguish it as a unique component in the system.

SYSTEMS THINKING SPOTLIGHT

modeling a system

02 ZOOM

LEVEL

EASY

Create a game about the fastest person you know.

EXPLANATION

There are many ways to express speed in games: fast music, fast enemies and racing spaces with a timer ticking away.

HINTS

In addition to using a fast avatar, try using a timer and timer bonuses to add an element of time pressure. Adding these system sprites not only makes the game more challenging, but also adds to the feeling of a quick, fast paced game.

SYSTEMS THINKING SPOTLIGHT

designing a system, system dynamics/interconnections.

03 FORTRESS IN THE SKY

LEVEL

EASY

Create a game that takes place in a fortress in the sky.

EXPLANATION

Fortresses are well defended with high walls and plenty of guards. They can be built so that each space inside is smaller and more secure the closer you get to the center.

HINTS

Games that take place in the sky often use heavy gravity to create a danger of falling. Try changing the gravity parameters to create a feeling of lightness—you'll find a dramatic change in the relationship between the components of avatar, ground, and sky.

SYSTEMS THINKING SPOTLIGHT

modeling a system, component relationships.

04
SUPERHERO

LEVEL

EASY

Create a game for a lost superhero.

EXPLANATION

Helping a superhero find their way home is no easy task! Well-designed spaces and helpful items can make their journey swifter.

HINTS

Maps can be useful if your superhero is lost in a maze. Imagine landmarks that might help your superhero or consider leaving a path of breadcrumbs—all are discrete components of a system.

SYSTEMS THINKING SPOTLIGHT

designing a system, of system structure.

05
FALLING FOREVER

LEVEL

EASY

Create a game about falling forever through time.

EXPLANATION

High vertical spaces or wrap-around spaces with unbounded edges can create a feeling of endlessness. Use timer bonuses to extend the plummet.

HINTS

What kind of a system expresses the concept of infinity? Try turning a small space into an infinite one that loops back on itself. If you were to imagine falling forever through time, what do you imagine yourself doing, seeing, and feeling?

SYSTEMS THINKING SPOTLIGHT

designing a system, system dynamics/interconnections.

06
DRIFT

LEVEL

EASY

Create a game about floating through an infinite landscape.

EXPLANATION

Use gravity, speed, and color to create a feeling of floating on air, or design a flying landscape.

HINTS

Imagine your avatar floating or drifting—what mechanics or relationships between system components might create this feeling in a game? How might a landscape be designed to feel like it goes on forever?

SYSTEMS THINKING SPOTLIGHT

designing a system, role of system structure

07
BFF

LEVEL

EASY

Create a game for your best friend.

EXPLANATION

Games can be used to paint a portrait of people you know.

HINTS

Think about attributes or adjectives you can use to describe your friend: fast, tricky, quiet, tough? What kind of personality does your best friend have (what kind of a system to all those adjectives add up to)? What kinds of activities does your best friend enjoy most? Build a game around these things.

SYSTEMS THINKING SPOTLIGHT

designing a system, considering a system's purpose or goal

08
DAZED AND CONFUSED

LEVEL

EASY

Create a game to make a player feel dazed and confused.

EXPLANATION

Sometimes it can be fun to design a game that is completely chaotic, where confusing the player is part of the fun.

HINTS

Try making a top down, wraparound game with unbounded edges: the player may have a hard time knowing where they are. Think about the attributes of the edge component of your system—how can you create relationships between the edge and an avatar that seem utterly confusing?

SYSTEMS THINKING SPOTLIGHT

designing a system,
role of system structure

09
SOUTH POLE

LEVEL

EASY

Create a game that takes place in a frozen landscape.

EXPLANATION

Sometimes game designers can be clever in how they choose to use sprites in their games. Cloud blocks, for example, can be used to create a level covered in snow. Glass blocks become sheets of ice.

HINTS

Imagine types of activities that could happen in a frozen landscape: ice-skating, sledding, snowball fights. Are there components like igloos, polar bears, or snowmen?

SYSTEMS THINKING SPOTLIGHT

modeling a system,
component relationships

10 BLACK AND WHITE

LEVEL

EASY

Create a game of black and white.

EXPLANATION

Black and white are colors in stark contrast to each other. One is the combination of all colors; the other contains none.

HINTS

What do the colors black and white make you think of? A newspaper? An old movie? A copy machine? Work with background and block components to create a distinctive look and feel for your game.

SYSTEMS THINKING SPOTLIGHT

designing a system,
role of system structure

11 FEEL THE RHYTHM

LEVEL

EASY

Create a game based on one of the soundtracks in the level editor.

EXPLANATION

You can create enemy patterns to sync with background music tracks. The visual design of the game can also capture the feeling.

HINTS

Movement style, turn direction, speed, and start direction are great tools for creating a rhythm. Choose a soundtrack and listen carefully. What player actions do you think would go well with this music? How might the music complement or contrast the system you've designed?

SYSTEMS THINKING SPOTLIGHT

designing a system,
component relationships

12 HAPPY BIRTHDAY

LEVEL

EASY

Create a game for a friend's birthday.

EXPLANATION

Birthdays involve many different kinds of objects and rituals, like singing "Happy Birthday," blowing out candles, and eating cake.

HINTS

Create a party atmosphere: consider the soundtrack, the decoration, and most of all, the fun as key components of your system. Puzzles can be enticing birthday gifts; blocks can be used to spell out a special birthday message.

SYSTEMS THINKING SPOTLIGHT

designing a system, considering
a system's purpose or goal

13
AMAZING RACE

LEVEL

EASY

Create a game about an amazing race.

EXPLANATION

The design of the racecourse can make the difference between winning and losing in games of speed.

HINTS

Timers create pressure and mark the beginning and ending of a race. Design a racecourse that is either long and flat or wide and windy. Think about making shortcuts and detours to give racers some choice in where they go in your system.

SYSTEMS THINKING SPOTLIGHT

designing a system, balancing feedback loops

14
DO NOT PASS!

LEVEL

EASY

Create a game with barriers and obstacles that you have to get by in order to win (or move to the next level).

EXPLANATION

Puzzles and complex enemy movements create obstacles that can help you control progress through a game.

HINTS

Think about ways of building obstacles into your system by stopping movement or causing sprites to change direction.

SYSTEMS THINKING SPOTLIGHT

designing a system, component relationships, balancing feedback loops

15
LEAGUE APPLICATION

LEVEL

MEDIUM

Apply to your favorite Gamestar district by making a game for it.

EXPLANATION

Knowing the genre or style of game specific to a district can help you fit in.

HINTS

Figure out which genres of games match each school: puzzles, racing games, mazes, and platformers—all represent very different kinds of systems. What is an innovative way to approach the design of a game that combines genres? A racing maze? A puzzle platformer?

SYSTEMS THINKING SPOTLIGHT

designing a system, component relationships, role of system structure

16 WRAPPED IN TIME

LEVEL

MEDIUM

Create a game about time travel.

EXPLANATION

What if time was like a loop? Where would you go? What would you do when you got to the past or future?

HINTS

Levels are parts of a system that can be used to express different time periods; doors and keys are components that can work like portals or black holes. Time travel is about exploration, too, so design the system of components making up your game space with many hidden features.

SYSTEMS THINKING SPOTLIGHT

modeling a system, system dynamics/interconnections

---

17 SPOOKY

LEVEL

MEDIUM

Create a game with unexpected encounters and misleading staircases

EXPLANATION

Designing surprise in a game can be accomplished in many ways. Game spaces can create paths to unexpected places, ghosts can appear from nowhere, and complex mazes can lead players astray.

HINTS

Random settings create variation in the behavior of components in a system, leading to unexpected outcomes. Adding randomness to spawning and movement is perfect way to create surprise. Similarly, wraparound spaces can lead to unexpected encounters with the enemy.

SYSTEMS THINKING SPOTLIGHT

designing a system, component relationships, system dynamics/interconnections

---

18 BEGINNING, MIDDLE, END

LEVEL

MEDIUM

Create a game with a beginning, middle and end. Earn bonus points for a surprise ending.

EXPLANATION

Levels can be used to create the beginning, middle, and end of a story, dividing your system into parts. Long or tall platformers can work like a scroll: begin the story at one edge and finish it at another.

HINTS

Entry and exit points are important indicators of progress in a system. Endings are often best communicated by reaching a goal—level complete!

SYSTEMS THINKING SPOTLIGHT

modeling a system, role of system structure, unintended consequences

19
JOURNEY TO FOREVER

LEVEL

MEDIUM

Create a game about a fantastic journey.

EXPLANATION

Games can tell the story of an incredible journey, one filled with excitement, conflict, action, and reward!

HINTS

Are you seeking something that has been lost, exploring hidden lands, or visiting imaginary friends? Imagine the types of things you might run into, or see along the way. Are these things the same from level to level? What are the components that would make a system feel fantastic?

SYSTEMS THINKING SPOTLIGHT

modeling a system, component relationships

20
THUD

LEVEL

MEDIUM

Create a game about feeling and falling like a heavy rock.

EXPLANATION

Gravity is a powerful force that pulls everything down, down, down. Heavy gravity means its pull is even more powerful.

HINTS

Create a space open enough in your system for objects to fall a long way. Can you create a level that makes it easy to fall down but difficult to climb up? How might you set the parameters of gravity in your system—very heavy or super light?

SYSTEMS THINKING SPOTLIGHT

modeling a system, role of system structure, system dynamics/interconnections

---

21
STRANGE PLANET

LEVEL

MEDIUM

Create a game about three weird things.

EXPLANATION

Weird things can be depicted in the design of a strange game space, series of events, or interaction between sprites.

HINTS

Randomness often leads to unexpected behavior, since random means unpredictable. What are some really weird things you have seen or experienced? Play with sprite parameters around randomness and movement to see if you can create some unusual interactions.

SYSTEMS THINKING SPOTLIGHT

designing a system, reinforcing feedback loops

22
RELAX

LEVEL

MEDIUM

Create a game for relaxation.

EXPLANATION

Relaxation is all about a lack of tension: soothing music, slow movement, and open-ended play.

HINTS

Think about the kinds of things you like to do after a long, tiring day. Make a game that is easy to play but is fun in a relaxing, meditative way. Perhaps the visuals or music in your system are soothing; or a small, repetitive activity mesmerizing. Design interesting spaces for your player to explore without the threat of enemies or time pressure.

SYSTEMS THINKING SPOTLIGHT

designing a system, balancing feedback loops

23
BRAVE AT
HEART

LEVEL

MEDIUM

Create a game for the brave at heart.

EXPLANATION

Players feel brave when they can successfully overcome obstacles. Bravery can come from how an avatar is designed to face off against an enemy.

HINTS

Design a game filled with challenges that must be overcome by taking chances. Players experience a feeling of risk in a system where there are no second chances or where they must act quickly without taking time to think. Consider designing a game with no extra lives, or with components that do high amounts of damage when touched.

SYSTEMS THINKING SPOTLIGHT

designing a system, system dynamics/interconnections

24
TUNNELS!
WAVES!
ELEVATORS!

LEVEL

MEDIUM

Create a game with tunnels, waves, and elevators.

EXPLANATION

Use movement speed and turn direction to create rhythmic waves with your enemies.

HINTS

Create unique wave patterns by modifying enemy movement parameters. This creates interesting and predictable relationships between components in your system. Vertical scrolling spaces are terrific for creating tunnels. Elevators can be placed throughout a level as part of an escape route.

SYSTEMS THINKING SPOTLIGHT

modeling a system, component relationships, system dynamics/interconnections

25
DIVE! DIVE! DIVE!

LEVEL
MEDIUM

Create a game that takes place 20,000 leagues under the sea.

EXPLANATION
What are you doing so deep under the sea? Searching for treasure? Hunting a sea monster? Gravity paired with the right combination of sprites can express a variety of underwater adventures.

HINTS
Experiment with the gravity setting to recreate the feeling of swimming. How can you use sprites to represent different underwater objects? What kinds of relationships do you need to create through movement and placement to model a deep sea paradise?

SYSTEMS THINKING SPOTLIGHT
modeling a system, component relationships, role of system structure

---

26
BRING IT ON!

LEVEL
MEDIUM

Create the hardest game possible that is still beatable.

EXPLANATION
A master game mechanic knows how to balance challenge, making games that are truly hard but also possible to win.

HINTS
Test out the use of timers to allow the player to finish just as time is about to run out. Build in traps that require players to be clever but give them enough clues to figure out the answer. Design the space in such a way that the player has to explore all parts of the system.

SYSTEMS THINKING SPOTLIGHT
designing a system, balancing feedback loops, reinforcing feedback loops

---

27
OPPOSITES ATTRACT

LEVEL
MEDIUM

Create a game about things that are opposite.

EXPLANATION
X vs. O, top vs. bottom, right vs. left, happy vs. sad, fast vs. slow. A game of opposites is a game of contradiction. Are friends really enemies? Is up really down?

HINTS
The different districts in Gamestar offer many options for creating patterns of opposites. Or think about pairing components with opposite colors, behaviors, or roles in your system—black vs. white, up vs. down, controlled vs. random, avatars vs. enemies.

SYSTEMS THINKING SPOTLIGHT
modeling a system, component relationships

28

ESCAPE FROM CELLBLOCK 9

LEVEL

MEDIUM

Create a game about a prison break.

EXPLANATION

Prisons are systems full of people, cells, locked doors and solid walls to prevent escape. They are designed to keep prisoners in—many of whom really want to get OUT.

HINTS

What components of the system work as obstacles preventing escape? Are there guards everywhere, or only in certain locations? Does a player need to search for and find the exits or find hidden keys? Is the prison a maze or a tower, a dungeon or an island?

SYSTEMS THINKING SPOTLIGHT

modeling a system, role of system structure, considering a system's purpose or goal

---

29

SOWING THE SEEDS

LEVEL

MEDIUM

Create a game that takes place in a garden.

EXPLANATION

What kinds of things grow in a garden? Flowers? Vegetables? Man-eating plants? Is the garden a community garden, a vegetable patch, or field of flowers?

HINTS

Use points or bonus points to represent seeds, flowers, or vegetables in your system. The grass and dirt blocks create a great foundation for you to build on. Spawning can create a feeling of change over time and allow for new patterns to emerge.

SYSTEMS THINKING SPOTLIGHT

modeling a system, component relationships, balancing feedback loops, reinforcing feedback loops

---

30

THE MESSAGE

LEVEL

MEDIUM

Create a game made up entirely of words that change.

EXPLANATION

Blocks on a grid can be used to embed secret messages in your game, or to tell a story with words built from sprites.

HINTS

Build a maze made of words—letterforms made of blocks are simple systems. Create a platformer that takes place in a city of letters. Use the matching blocks to create a word scramble. Think. Write. Communicate.

SYSTEMS THINKING SPOTLIGHT

designing a system, component relationships, unintended consequences

Card 31

31 NEXT STOP JUPITER

LEVEL

HARD

Create a game about a virtual tour of the solar system.

EXPLANATION

Earthlings battling hostile life forms or tourists tracking hidden constellations? Whatever your take, the design of space in your game will be important.

HINTS

Scrolling spaces can offer a powerful canvas for intergalactic exploration. Use short-term goals to keep your players excited throughout the journey and design a system full of space-like hazards.

SYSTEMS THINKING SPOTLIGHT

modeling a system, identifying components, identifying behaviors, role of system structure

Card 32

32 SNEAKY PANTS

LEVEL

HARD

Create a game that would make the player feel sneaky.

EXPLANATION

A feeling of being sneaky can be achieved through movement style: hiding behind obstacles or moving slowly while being hidden from view.

HINTS

Create opportunities to play hide and seek. Consider ways of making the player feel clever in your system by giving them clues the enemy can't see.

SYSTEMS THINKING SPOTLIGHT

designing a system, considering a system's purpose or goal, component relationships

Card 33

33 THIS OR THAT

LEVEL

HARD

Create a game that can be played two different ways.

EXPLANATION

System sprites can define certain ways of playing a game, whether it's racking up points or racing through space to beat the timer.

HINTS

Design a game space with different points of entry and exit. What combination of components can be used to create different goals or choices within the system?

SYSTEMS THINKING SPOTLIGHT

designing a system, component relationships, looking at a system from multiple perspectives

34
HOME

LEVEL

HARD

Create a game about your neighborhood.

EXPLANATION

Spaces in the real world can be great inspiration for games.

HINTS

Think about who lives in your neighborhood and how you would represent them as a system of interrelated parts. Ask, "What is unique about my neighborhood? How can I model the system in the form of a game?" Think about what people like to do there, how they move around, and the places you like to go.

SYSTEMS THINKING SPOTLIGHT

modeling a system, identifying components, identifying behaviors, nested systems

---

35
TOPSY TURVY

LEVEL

HARD

Create a game in which a world goes topsy-turvy.

EXPLANATION

Imagine a world that is topsy-turvy. What do you think would be going on there? What would it look like and how would it make you feel?

HINTS

Try using a wraparound space and ghosts as components. Randomness can help lend a chaotic edge to the behavior of your system. The design of a space that looks the same right side up and upside down is sure to confuse.

SYSTEMS THINKING SPOTLIGHT

designing a system, considering a system's purpose or goal, component relationships

---

36
FORBIDDEN FOREST

LEVEL

HARD

Create a game about a haunted forest.

EXPLANATION

Design a game to capture the isolation and creepiness of a forbidden forest.

HINTS

Design a system full of unexpected outcomes by exploring randomness, patterns, and complex relationships between components. What types of things make up your system: creepy crawlies, caves, or strange weather?

SYSTEMS THINKING SPOTLIGHT

modeling a system, designing behaviors, component relationships, nested systems

37
VOLCANO!

LEVEL

HARD

Create a game that takes place inside of an erupting volcano.

EXPLANATION

Volcanoes are filled with hot, liquid lava. They can be explosive and dangerous.

HINTS

Imagine a story placing your player inside the volcano. Is the player a scientist studying the volcano and its patterns of eruption over time? Has he or she fallen inside? Is someone guarding the volcano? Might it contain secret treasure?

SYSTEMS THINKING SPOTLIGHT

modeling a system, component relationships, system dynamics/ interconnections

---

38
SAFARI

LEVEL

HARD

Create a game about being on a jungle safari.

EXPLANATION

Game spaces can be designed to model different types of terrain. Level parameters related to edge bounding, scrolling, and gravity are all useful tools. Imagine the kinds of things you would see on a jungle safari—creatures, trees, and people.

HINTS

Think about all of the components that make up the system that is the jungle— landscape, weather, plants, animals, and humans? What might be the challenge of moving through a jungle? What obstacles and surprises might you encounter in the system?

SYSTEMS THINKING SPOTLIGHT

modeling a system, component relationships, role of system structure

---

39
THE FOUR SEASONS

LEVEL

HARD

Create a game about the change of seasons.

EXPLANATION

Winter, spring, summer, or fall, seasons express feelings, land- scapes, weather, and the passing of time.

HINTS

Create a system that shows the cyclical nature of seasons. Use more than one level to show changes in a landscape over time. Think about the role soundtracks can play in evoking a mood or style.

SYSTEMS THINKING SPOTLIGHT

modeling a system, component relationships, system dynamics/ interconnections

40
SUNRISE TO SUNSET

LEVEL

HARD

Create a game that starts in the morning and ends at night.

EXPLANATION

Changes in the day can be expressed through a change in mechanic (do you do different things in the morning than at night?), the use of backgrounds, music, or a sequence of levels.

HINTS

Use a horizontal scrolling space that starts and ends with dark colored blocks to represent the sunrise and sunset. Use the brightest colored blocks to the midday sun. Consider time as a core component in your system.

SYSTEMS THINKING SPOTLIGHT

modeling a system, identifying components, identifying behaviors

41
TICK TOCK CLOCK

LEVEL

HARDCORE

Create a game that works like a clock.

EXPLANATION

Use enemy movement patterns to represent the parts of a working clock. The relationship between seconds, minutes, and hours can be expressed in the design of the game space.

HINTS

Consider what kinds of components make up a clock as a time-keeping system. How might this system be recreated in a game? Think about various materials used to create clocks: sand through an hourglass, numbers on a clockface, light and shadow on a sundial—and use blocks to model their material properties.

SYSTEMS THINKING SPOTLIGHT

modeling a system, identifying components, identifying behaviors, balancing feedback loops

42
STORY CENTRAL

LEVEL

HARDCORE

Create a game based on the plot of your favorite movie.

EXPLANATION

In a narrative, the plot is the primary sequence of events. Games can have plots too, which can unfold within a single level or across several.

HINTS

Pick a movie and choose a sequence of events that describe the action of the film. Game descriptions, intro and outro screens are all useful components in helping to tell the story.

SYSTEMS THINKING SPOTLIGHT

designing a system, component relationships, system dynamics/interconnections

43
HIDDEN TREASURES

LEVEL

HARDCORE

Create a game about plundering ancient Mayan treasures.

EXPLANATION

Treasure hunters rely on tricks of the trade: code breaking, puzzle solving, and outsmarting clever enemies.

HINTS

Create a challenging puzzle your treasure seeker will have to solve in order to advance through the system. Doors and keys can be useful components to make sure the treasure is well guarded. Ruins can be made from blocks of alabaster.

SYSTEMS THINKING SPOTLIGHT

designing a system, component relationships, system dynamics/interconnections

44
KALEIDOSCOPE

LEVEL

HARDCORE

Create a game that is like a kaleidoscope.

EXPLANATION

Kaleidoscopes work with mirrors and color to create patterns. Games can be designed with a similar idea, especially those where the spaces scroll.

HINTS

Play around with the idea of constantly changing patterns—patterns of blocks, enemies, and items. Imagine how patterns in a system can be altered through player interaction.

SYSTEMS THINKING SPOTLIGHT

modeling a system, identifying components, identifying behaviors, system dynamics/interconnections

45
TURNABOUT TALE

LEVEL

HARDCORE

Create a game where the character is moving backwards through a story.

EXPLANATION

What can be done better backwards—spelling your name or reading a book? The elements are the same, only the order is different.

HINTS

Design the first level to be the most difficult and the last level the easiest. The intro and outro labels can be very useful, allowing the designers to reverse the usual flow of information in a system.

SYSTEMS THINKING SPOTLIGHT

modeling a system, component relationships, role of system structure

GAMING THE SYSTEM CHALLENGE CARDS	GAMING THE SYSTEM CHALLENGE CARDS	GAMING THE SYSTEM CHALLENGE CARDS

46
PLAGUE BUSTERS

LEVEL

HARDCORE

Create a game about controlling or releasing a plague.

EXPLANATION

A plague will spread and infect others if it is not controlled.

HINTS

Enemy sprites that spawn or enemy generators are components that can be used to create a virus spreading out of control. Control the pacing of the outbreak by controlling the speed of spawning and enemy sprites. Plan for unexpected interactions between components and ways of bringing those interactions under control.

SYSTEMS THINKING SPOTLIGHT

modeling a system, system dynamics/interconnections, reinforcing and balancing feedback loops

47
PRISM PLANET

LEVEL

HARDCORE

Create a game that works like a prism.

EXPLANATION

Metaphorically, a prism can refer to anything that is used to look at the world differently. Like a friend with interesting opinions, a prism separates colors by bending them by different degrees.

HINTS

Color can be used to express the idea of a prism, as can a story that has a special point of view, or more than one! Pay special attention to the relationships between parts in your system, which can model the scientific principles behind color and light.

SYSTEMS THINKING SPOTLIGHT

modeling a system, system dynamics/interconnections

48
EXCELLENT ADVENTURE

LEVEL

HARDCORE

Create a game about traveling through time to a different historical era.

EXPLANATION

Why are you traveling through history? Are you trying to change the past? Are you chasing someone? Are you trying to trace your family tree?

HINTS

Your choice of block sprites might depend on the historical era you choose to model as a system. Use the alabaster block for ancient Rome, the dirt block for the Stone Age, and the cement block for the middle Ages.

SYSTEMS THINKING SPOTLIGHT

designing a system, modeling a system

REFERENCES

Baafi, E., & Millner, A. (2011). Modkit: A toolkit for tinkering with tangibles and connecting communities. *Proceedings of Tangible, Embedded, and Embodied Interaction* (TEI). doi 10.1145/1935701.1935783.

Brown, A. L. (1992). Design experiments: Theoretical and methodological challenges in creating complex interventions in classroom settings. *Journal of the Learning Sciences* 2 (2): 141–178.

Brown, Gordon S. (1990). The genesis of the system thinking program at the Orange Grove Middle School, Tucson, Arizona. Personal report. 6301 N. Calle de Adelita, Tucson, AZ 85718: March 1.

Buechley, Leah. (2006). A construction kit for electronic textiles. In *Proceedings of the IEEE International Symposium on Wearable Computers (ISWC)*, 83–90.

Colella, V. (2000). Participatory simulations: Building collaborative understanding through immersive dynamic modeling. *Journal of the Learning Sciences* 9 (4): 471–500.

Colella, V. S., E. Klopfer, and M. Resnick. (2001). *Adventures in modeling: Exploring complex dynamic systems with Starlogo.* New York: Teachers College Press.

Danish, J., K. Peppler, D. Phelps, and D. Washington. (2011). Life in the hive: Supporting inquiry into complexity within the zone of proximal development. *Journal of Science Education and Technology* 20 (5): 454–467.

Draper, F. (1989). Letter to Jay Forrester. Personal communication, Orange Grove Junior High School, 1911 E. Orange Grove Rd., Tucson, AZ 85718. May 2.

Goldstone, R. L., and U. Wilensky. (2008). Promoting transfer through complex systems principles. *Journal of the Learning Sciences* 17:465–516.

Hmelo-Silver, C., and M. G. Pfeffer. (2004). Comparing expert and novice understanding of a complex system from the perspective of structures, behaviors, and functions. *Cognitive Science* 28 (1): 127–138.

Hmelo-Silver, C., R. Jordan, L. Liu, and E. Chernobilsky. (2011). Representational tools for understanding complex computer-supported collaborative learning environments. *Computer-Supported Collaborative Learning Series* 12 (Part 1): 83–106. doi:10.1007/978-1-4419-7710-6_4.

Kafai, Y. B. (2006). Constructionism. In K. Sawyer (Ed.), *Cambridge Handbook of the Learning Sciences* (35–46). New York: Cambridge University Press.

Lenhart, A., and M. Madden. (2007). *Social networking websites and teens: An overview.* Washington, DC: Pew Internet and American Life Project.

Lyneis, D. (2000). Bringing system dynamics to a school near you: Suggestions for introducing and sustaining system dynamics in K–12 education. International System Dynamics Society Conference. Bergen, Norway.

Meadows, D. (1999). *Leverage points: Places to intervene in a system.* Hartland, VT: Sustainability Institute.

Papert, S. (1980). *Mindstorms: Children, computers, and powerful ideas.* New York: Basic Books.

Papert, S., and I. Harel. (1991). *Constructionism.* New York: Ablex Publishing Corporation. http://www.papert.org/articles/SituatingConstructionism.html.

Peppler, K. A., and Y. B. Kafai. (2007). From SuperGoo to Scratch: Exploring creative digital media production in informal learning. *Learning, Media, and Technology* 32 (2): 149–166.

Resnick, M. (2007). All I really need to know (about creative thinking) I learned (by studying how children learn) in kindergarten. *Proceedings of the 6th ACM SIGCHI Conference on Creativity & Cognition.* doi 10.1145/1254960.1254961.

Resnick, M., et al. (2009). Scratch: Programming for all. *Communications of the ACM* 52 (11): 60–67.

Rusk, N., M. Resnick, and S. Cooke. (2009). Origins and guiding principles of the Computer Clubhouse. In Y. Kafai, K. Peppler, and R. Chapman (Eds.), *The Computer Clubhouse: Constructionism and creativity in youth communities.* New York: Teachers College Press.

Salen, K. (2007). Gaming literacies: A game design study in action. *Journal of Educational Multimedia and Hypermedia* 16 (3): 301–322.

Salen, K. (2008). Toward an ecology of gaming. In *The ecology of games: Connecting youth, games, and learning.*, ed. K. Salen. Cambridge, MA: MIT Press.

Salen, K., R. Torres, R. Rufo-Tepper, A. Shapiro, and L. Wolozin. (2010). *Quest to learn: Growing a school for digital kids.* Cambridge, MA: MIT Press.

Sweeney, L. (2001). *When a butterfly sneezes: A guide for helping kids explore interconnections in our world through favorite stories.* Waltham, MA: Pegasus Communications.

Wilensky, U. (1999). NetLogo. [Computer Program]. Center for Connected Learning and Computer-Based Modeling. Northwestern University, Evanston, IL.

Wilensky, U., and M. Resnick. (1999). Thinking in levels: A dynamic systems perspective to making sense of the world. *Journal of Science Education and Technology* 8 (1): 3–19.

INDEX

INTERCONNECTIONS CURRICULA SUMMARY SHEET:
GAMING THE SYSTEM

WHAT IS THE INTERCONNECTIONS CURRICULA?

Interconnections: Understanding Systems through Digital Design is a series of curricula that support students to develop critical 21st century skills—systems thinking and digital design—by engaging in rich project-based learning using the latest technologies.

WHAT'S SYSTEMS THINKING, AND WHY IS IT IMPORTANT FOR MY STUDENTS?

As the world gets more complex and interconnected, we need to help our kids to understand and positively impact the dizzying number of systems around them. Systems thinking is a set of ideas and practices that allow kids to see through the "lens" of systems: how to take a "big picture" view of complex social structures and technologies, how to see the patterns and dynamics that drive systems, how to understand that the whole is usually greater than the sum of its parts.

HOW IS DIGITAL DESIGN DIFFERENT FROM OTHER USES OF EDUCATIONAL TECHNOLOGY?

Digital design is all about getting students the skills they need in order to be innovative, creative, and entrepreneurial thinkers. Rather than educational technologies that replicate a consumer mentality around learning, dumping information into students' brains, digital design activities put them in the driver's seat, having them come up with the ways technology can look in the world and preparing them for a world that increasingly expects them to engage in creative processes.

GAME DESIGN, REALLY?

There are lots of great reasons we've found in our work to use game design as the foundation for a classroom curriculum. Games are incredibly engaging, are deeply part of youth culture, and can be leveraged to get students excited about entering into some pretty important academic practices: giving and getting feedback, revising drafts, making arguments, problem solving, and more.

DOES THIS ALIGN TO STANDARDS?

Yes! All the Interconnections curricula have been aligned to the Common Core State Standards in areas including language arts, history and science, as well as the Next Generation Science Standards.

HOW MUCH TIME DOES THIS TAKE?

The *Gaming the System* curriculum is designed to take about 20–30 hours overall, but of course can and will be adapted to fit your students' needs and abilities, as well as your school culture. This means that we fully expect that you might take certain parts and extend them, cut other parts, or repurpose them to fit existing units of study.